D0990384

The Basic Trends of Our Times

The Basic Trends of Our Times

PITIRIM A. SOROKIN

COLLEGE & UNIVERSITY PRESS · Publishers
NEW HAVEN, CONN.

Foreword

These essays outline, in terms comprehensible to the intelligent lay-reader, the basic trends of our time and sketch the frontlines of that gigantic struggle which is taking place in the mind, soul, and body of all mankind and in all social groups, large and small.

The first essay delineates the three major, basic trends. The second essay enlarges upon the first trend —the shift and diffusion of creative leadership from the West to the East—and gives a diagnosis and prognosis of East-West relationships. The third portrays all three basic trends as they are reflected in the mutual convergence of the United States and USSR to become an intermediary type.

The fourth essay deals with the uniformity occurring in all great catastrophes, namely, with religious and moral polarization as it manifests itself in today's crisis of mankind. Finally, the fifth essay sketches a new field of research—the field of the mysterious energy of creative, unselfish love which is bound to play a greatly increased role in the future life of humanity if it avoids new suicidal wars. Together, these trends are the most important of our time, all other trends being merely partial manifestations of these basic processes.

PITIRIM A. SOROKIN

Acknowledgments

I wish to thank the following institutions at which these addresses were delivered and the publications in which they appeared:

The 18th and the 19th International Congresses of Sociology (at Nürnberg and Mexico City, respectively) at whose plenary sessions the following essays were read: "Three Basic Trends of Our Time," "The Mysterious Energy of Love," and "Mutual Convergence of the United States and the USSR to the Mixed Intermediary Type."

The editors of the *Akten des XVIII, Internationalen Soziologenkongresses* (Meisenheim am Glan, Verlag Anton Hain KG, vol. I, 1961) the *Mémoire du XIXe Congrès International de Sociologie* (Mexico, D. F., vol. III, 1961), and *Main Currents in Modern Thought* (vol. 16, 1960), who published these essays.

Colby College where the address "Diagnosis and Prognosis of East-West Relationship" was given in its distinguished lectures series for 1963.

Princeton Theological Seminary where the essay "Religious and Moral Polarization of Our Time" was delivered in 1963 at the Seminary's Sesquicentennial History Department Conference on Religion and Social Life.

Dedication of this book to Professors Gordon W. Allport and Carle C. Zimmerman is a token of my deep appreciation of their friendship and of their important contributions to the psychosocial sciences.

Contents

The Basic Trends of Our Times

Three Basic Trends of our Time

The three most important trends of our time are, first, a shift of the creative leadership of mankind from Europe and the European West, where it has been centered during the last five centuries, to a wider area of the Pacific and the Atlantic, particularly the Americas, Asia, and Africa; second, a continued disintegration of the hitherto predominant sensate man, culture, society, and system of values; third, the emergence and slow growth of the first components of a new—integral—order, system of values, and type of personality.

1. THE SHIFT OF CREATIVE LEADERSHIP We all know that creative leadership, on a small and large scale, in narrow and broad fields of activity, shifts in the course of time from place to place, group to group, institution to institution, country to country. Thus, in the days of William James, Josiah Royce, Peirce, Palmer, and Münsterberg, the Harvard department of philosophy was certainly the leading one of all the philosophy departments of American universities. With the death of these philosophers the Harvard department lost its pre-eminence and the philosophy departments of other universities assumed the leadership. Some thirty years ago the University of Chicago undoubtedly had the leading department of sociology in this country. Eventually it lost this leading role. The same applies to other departments of universities and to any kind of leadership. Some seventy years ago New England was the center of the textile and other industries. Later, the centers of the textile and steel and other industries moved to other regions of the United States. From 800 to 1600 A.D., Italy made some twenty-

five to forty-one per cent of all the scientific discoveries and inventions in Europe; from 1726 to the present the Italian share dwindled to approximately two or four per cent. The United States contributed only one and one-tenth per cent of the total discoveries and inventions in the period of 1726-50; this share increased to twenty-five and three-tenths per cent for the period 1900-08; at the present time it is still greater.*

History tells us that at one time the great center of political power was in Egypt; at another period it shifted to Babylon or Persia, then to India or China, then to Rome or Europe; and within Europe it continued to shift from nation to nation. Likewise, the great centers of musical creativity in Europe were at one period in Sparta; then in Rome and Milan; then, after the medieval period, in Italy and France, the Netherlands and England, Austria and Germany; and, finally, in Russia, Norway, Finland, and the United States. For the last ten centuries the creative centers of the economic empires of Europe were in Spain, Portugal, and Italy, then in the Netherlands, France, England, Austria, and Germany; now the center has shifted to the United States and Russia.

These examples show clearly what is meant by the shift of creative centers of leadership.

Most indicative of this mobility is the shift in the creative center of human history or in the leadership of the whole of mankind.

Until the fourteenth century, or thereabout, the creative leadership of mankind was held by the people and nations of Asia and Africa. While our forefathers in the West still had a most primitive life and culture, in Africa and Asia the great civilizations—Egyptian, Babylonian, Iranic, Sumerian, Hittite, Hindu, Chinese, Mediterranean (Creto-Mycenaean,

---

* See the detailed statistics of scientific discoveries and inventions made by various Western countries from 700 to 1908 A.D. in P. A., Sorokin, *Social and Cultural Dynamics* (New York: Bedminster Press, 1962), II, 141ff.; P. Sorokin, *Society, Culture and Personality* (New York: Cooper Square Publishers, 1962), pp. 570-72.

Greco-Roman, Arabic) and others—emerged, grew and fluctuated for millennia in their repeated blossoming and decay. The Western—Euro-American—peoples were the latest to assume the creative leadership of mankind. They have carried this torch only during the last five or six centuries.

During this short period they have discharged their creative mission brilliantly, especially in the fields of science, technology, sensate fine arts, politics, and economics. At the present time, however, European monopolistic leadership can be considered almost ended. The present and the future history of mankind is already being staged on the much larger scene of the Asian-African-American-European cosmopolitan theater. And the stars of the next acts of the great historical drama are going to be— besides Europe, the Americas, and Russia—the renascent great cultures of India, China, Japan, Indonesia, and the Islamic world. This epochal shift has already started and has manifested itself in the dissolution of great European empires like the British and the French, in the decreasing political and cultural influence of Europe in international relationships, in the shift in creativity of several European nations to other continents: the Anglo-Saxon to the United States, Canada, and Australia; the Spanish and Portuguese to Latin America; the creative growth of Asiatic Russia in comparison with its European part, and so on. A still stronger manifestation of this shift is the unquestionable renaissance of the great cultures of Asia and Africa: the Indian, the Chinese, the Japanese, the Indonesian, the Arabic, the Jewish and others. The successful liberation of these nations from colonial servitude—the rapid growth of their political and social independence, of their influence in international affairs, of their scientific and technological development (including their increase of Nobel and similar prize winners) ; a successful diffusion of their religious, philosophical, ethical, artistic, and cultural values in the Western world; and many other phenomena display the beginning of this renaissance. All this and much other evidence make fairly certain the indication of a shift in the creative leadership of man-kind from a monopolistic domination by Europe to the Amer-icas, Asia, and Africa. This shift is pregnant with momen-tous changes in all areas of all cultures and in the social life of all nations. Its effects upon the future history of mankind are going to be incomparably greater than those of the alliances and disalliances of the Western governments and ruling groups. Such is the first basic sociocultural trend of the last few decades. (For further information on this trend see my subsequent essay "Diagnosis and Prognosis of East-West Relationships.")

2. SENSATE, IDEATIONAL, AND INTEGRAL SOCIOCULTURAL ORDERS

The other two trends, a continued decay of the sensate socio-cultural system of the West and an emergence and growth of a new—integral—sociocultural order, are possibly still more im-portant for the present and future of mankind. In order to reveal the full meaning of this statement I must define these terms.

Some thirty years ago I made a detailed diagnosis of the present state of Western culture and society, with a forecast of the coming trends, including repeated warnings about the im-minent terrible wars, bloody revolutions, misery, and "libera-tion" in man of "the worst of the beasts." In summarized form this diagnosis runs as follows:

> Every important aspect of the life, the organization, and the culture of Western society is in extraordinary crisis. . . . Its body and mind are sick. . . . We are seemingly between two epochs: the dying sensate (secular) culture of our magnificent yesterday and the coming (new) culture of the creative tomorrow. We are living, thinking, and acting at the end of a brilliant six-hundred-year-long sensate day. The oblique rays of the sun still illumine the glory of the passing epoch. But the light is fading, and in the deepening shadows it becomes more and more difficult to see clearly and to orient ourselves safely in the confusions of twilight. The night of the transitory period begins to loom before

us, with its nightmares, frightening shadows, and heart-rending horrors. Beyond it, however, the dawn of a new great culture is probably waiting to greet the men of the future.

Despite inimical criticism of my diagnosis by the gaudily optimistic opinion of the 1920's, my forecasts during the last thirty years turned out to be correct. So far, history has revealed itself according to my predictions.

Since the transitional state of the present Euro-American culture and society largely determines their essential features, it is advisable to outline more precisely the nature of the crisis they are in at the present time.

Briefly, the main elements of the crisis are as follows: It consists of a disintegration in the sensate form of our culture, society, and way of life, which has been dominant in the Western world during the last five centuries; the crisis involves all areas of this sensate culture and society; in this sense it is total, epochal, and the greatest of all the crises of the Western world's history.

Sensate Culture

The sensate form of culture and society is based upon the ultimate principle that true reality and value are sensory and that beyond the reality and values which we can see, hear, smell, touch and taste there is no other reality and no real values.

The whole system of sensate culture represents an articulation and "materialization" of this ultimate principle in its science and philosophy, its modicum of religion, its law and ethics, its economics and politics, its fine arts, and its social institutions. This basic principle becomes also the main determinant of the dominant mentality, aspirations, and way of life of sensate society. Quite consistently, sensate culture makes the testimony of our senses the criterion of what is true and what is false. It intensely cultivates scientific knowledge of the physical and biological properties of sensory reality, which contributes little creative thought to the fields of supersensory religion and theology.

Although sensate society is quite successful in producing many technological inventions aimed at increasing the bodily comforts of sensory life, it is not successful in yielding effective techniques for the transfiguration of souls and for the "production" of the supersensory values of the Kingdom of God. While it greatly favors the development of materialist, empiricist, positivist, and other sensory philosophies, it disfavors the cultivation of idealistic, mystical, and supersensory systems of philosophy. Despite its lip-service to the values of the Kingdom of God, it cares mainly about the sensory values of wealth, health, bodily comfort, sensual pleasures, and lust for power and fame. Its dominant ethic is invariably utilitarian and hedonistic. It views all ethical and legal precepts as mere man-made conventions, perfectly relative and changeable. Its politics and economics are also decisively utilitarian and hedonistic. And as we shall see, its fine arts are marked by similar sensory characteristics.

Sensate form emerged in Western culture at the end of the twelfth century and subsequently, after the fifteenth century, became dominant, supplanting the preceding religious or ideational form which prevailed during the medieval period of Western culture and society from about the seventh to the thirteenth century.

Ideational Culture

The ideational culture and society of the Middle Ages were based upon, and articulated in all their aspects the ultimate principle that the true reality, or value, is the supersensory and superrational God and his Kingdom as defined in the Christian Credo; while sensory reality, or value, is either a mere mirage or even something negative and sinful. Moreover, ideational culture believed in God's revelations as the criterion of truth and disbelieved in the testimony of the senses. Accordingly, ideational culture cares little about scientific study of sensory phenomena or about inventing technological gadgets; since the whole sensory world is a mere mirage, such activities are but a waste of time and energy, an investigation of the mere shadows of reality and value.

Therefore, ideational culture is uncreative in the field of science and technology, for it concentrates its cognitive energy on a study of the Kingdom of God and on a realization of values during man's short earthly pilgrimage to eternity. St. Augustine's *"Deum et animam scire cupio. Nihilne plus? Nihil omnino* (I want to know God and soul. Nothing more? Absolutely nothing.) admirably expresses this property of ideational culture. For this reason, it is creative in the field of religion: Theology logically becomes the queen of sciences, and science functions only as a handmaid of religion. Only idealistic, mystical, and suprasensory philosophies blossom within it, while materialistic, mechanistic, empiricist, positivist, and other sensory philosophies in this type of culture have no success. It is concerned primarily with the salvation of souls and with the values of God's Kingdom, and views as sin and temptation concern for material and sensory values. Its verities and its ethical and legal precepts are regarded as God's revealed commandments, universal and unconditional in their truth and binding power, its government is conspicuously theocratic and its spiritual authority has supremacy over secular powers. In addition, its economics is conditioned by its religious and moral commandments.

Finally, sensate and ideational cultures have entirely different types of fine arts, each created in accordance with the ultimate principle of the culture. The two types of art differ from each other in their subject matter as well as in their styles.

In accordance with the ultimate principles of ideational culture, the subject matter of ideational art is the supersensory Kingdom of God. Its "heroes" are God, angels, saints, and the soul, as well as the mysteries of Creation, Incarnation, Redemption, and other transcendental events. It is religious art, through and through. It pays little attention to persons, objects, and events of the sensory world. Therefore, in painting there is little landscape, genre, still life, or portraiture of actual persons. Its object is not to amuse, to entertain, or to give pleasure, but to bring the believer into a closer harmony with God. Its art is sacred and does not admit any sensualism, eroticism, satire, comedy, or caricature. Its emotional tone is pious, ethereal, and ascetic.

The dominant style of ideational art is symbolic, being a mere visible, audible, or sensory sign for the invisible or supersensory world of values. Since God and supersensory realities do not have any specific material forms, they cannot be perceived and depicted naturalistically; they can only be denoted symbolically. The signs of the dove, anchor, or olive branch in early Christian catacombs were visible symbols of the values of the invisible world of God. Immersed in an eternal transcendental world, ideational art is static, hieratic, externally simple, even archaic, devoid of sensory trimmings, pomp, and ostentation. Being an art of the communion of the human soul with its God and with itself, it does not need professional mediator-artists and is the creation of an anonymous collectivity of believers conversing with God and with their own souls.

We all know that the supreme examples of medieval architecture are the great cathedrals devoted to God. Their external forms—the cruciform foundation, the dome or the spire, and almost every architectural and sculptural detail—are symbolic. They are truly the Bible in stone. Medieval sculpture, in turn, is entirely religious and represents the Old and the New Testaments "frozen" in stone, clay, wood, or marble. Medieval painting is, moreover, a pictorial representation of these Testaments; it is almost entirely symbolic and otherworldly. Medieval literature is derived mainly from the Bible. Medieval music consists of the Ambrosian, the Gregorian, and other plain chants, with their Kyrie eleison, Agnus-Dei, Credo, and semi-religious pilgrims' chants. Externally it is unisonous, ethereal, devoid of any sensate embellishment. It is indeed the music of the communion of the human soul with God. Religious services and ceremonies are the main form of medieval drama. This art was not designed for the market, for purposes of profit, for fame, for popularity, or for sensual enjoyment. It was created, as Theophilus said, *"nec humane laudis amore, nec temporalis premii cupiditate . . . sed in augmentum honoris et gloriae nominis Dei "* (not for human love of praise, nor for greed of worldly reward, but in the enhancement of honor and for the glory of the name of God). In brief, the dominant medieval art was a truly great ideational art.

In accordance with the ultimate principle of sensate culture, sensate art lives and moves entirely within the empirical world of the senses. Empirical landscape, genre, objects, events, and adventures, empirical portraiture, and sensory values are its subject matter. Political and business bosses, farmers, workers, housewives, girls, and other human beings are its models. The aim of sensate art is to afford refined sensual enjoyment, relaxation, stimulation of tired nerves, amusement, pleasure, and entertainment. For this reason it must be sensational, passionate, pathetic, sensual, and incessantly new. In the concupiscence and eroticism of its overripe phase, it is divorced from religion, morals, often even from science, philosophy, and other values, and calls itself "art for art's sake." Since it must entertain, it widely uses caricature, satire, comedy, farce, debunking, ridicule, and similar means. At its overripe stage, it becomes eclectic and presents in its exhibits and best-sellers an atrocious concoction of trivia.

Its style is naturalistic, visual, free from any supersensory symbolism. It reproduces empirical phenomena as they look, sound, smell, or otherwise appear to our sense organs. It is dynamic in its very nature, in its emotionalism, its violent passions, actions, and scenes. It has to be incessantly changing in its succession of fads and fashions, because otherwise it becomes boring and unenjoyable. It is the art of external show, dressed up for exhibition. Since it does not symbolize any supersensory value, it stands and falls by its physical appearance, like a glamor girl. To retain its charm, it has to make lavish use of "lipstick and powder," pomp and circumstance, colossality, stunning technique and other means of external adornment. It is an art of professional artists catering to their patrons and to a passive public and, at its overripe stage, to the demands of the market and the various commercial dealers in art.

Integral Culture

Once in a while a third basic type of culture and fine arts, an intermediary between the sensate and the ideational, appears and blossoms for a comparatively short time. Its ultimate principle proclaims that the true reality-value is an Infinite Manifold which has supersensory, rational, and sensory forms inseparable from one another. This type of culture can be called integral. All its compartments and its social life articulate this principle. It pays attention to the empirical as well as the superempirical aspects of the true reality-value. Science as well as philosophy and theology begin to blossom in it, and they harmoniously cooperate with one another. The subjects of its fine arts are partly supersensory and partly empirical, but only in the noblest and most sublime aspects of sensory reality. Its heroes are partly gods, partly heroic human beings at their best. It is an art intentionally blind to everything vulgar, debasing, and ugly in the empirical world of the senses. It ennobles the ignoble, beautifies the ugly, rejuvenates the old, and immortalizes the mortal. Its style is partly symbolic and allegorical, partly realistic and naturalistic. Its emotional tone is serene, calm, and imperturbable. The artist here is merely *primus inter pares* of the community of which he is a member.

Three Basic Trends of our Time

Each of these three types of culture and fine arts has been realized several times: among preliterate tribes, in Ancient Egypt, Babylon, Iran, India, China, Greece and Rome, and in the Western world. In the life-history of Greco-Roman-Western culture and art, the dominant form of Greek culture and fine arts from the ninth to the sixth century B.C. was ideational; from the second half of the sixth to the end of the fourth century B.C. they were predominantly integral; during the subsequent centuries Greco-Roman culture and art became predominantly sensate; after the third century A.D. they disintegrated into an eclectic mixture of different types until this eclecticism was replaced, after the sixth century, by Christian ideational culture and fine art, which maintained its domination up to the end of the twelfth century.

At the end of the twelfth century, ideational art, as well as the whole ideational culture, began to disintegrate and a new sensate culture and art emerged and started to grow. In the thirteenth century these two currents met and produced the marvelous European integral culture and art of the thirteenth and fourteenth centuries. At the end of the fifteenth century the sensate type of culture and most of the European fine arts (except music, whose integral type maintained its slight preeminence almost to the nineteenth century) grew to be dominant and continued its domination until the end of the nineteenth century. During the centuries of its domination sensate culture progressed unprecedentedly in science, technology, economics, and politics; and it created a vast treasury of the magnificent masterpieces of sensate music, painting, sculpture, literature, and drama. However, at the end of the nineteenth century this creative culture began to show the symptoms of fatigue and disintegration.*

* See for a detailed development and documentation of this sketch, P. A. Sorokin, *Social and Cultural Dynamics,* 4 vols. (New York: Bedminster Press, 1962).

*The Explosion of Wars, Revolutions, and Crimes as a
Consequence of the Disintegration of Sensate Order*

In the twentieth century the magnificent sensate house of
Western man began to deteriorate rapidly and then to crumble.
There was, among other things, a disintegration of its moral,
legal, and other values which, from within, control and guide
the behavior of individuals and groups. When human beings
cease to be controlled by deeply interiorized religious, ethical,
aesthetic and other values, individuals and groups become the
victims of crude power and fraud as the supreme controlling
forces of their behavior, relationship, and destiny. In such circumstances, man turns into a human animal driven mainly by
his biological urges, passions, and lust. Individual and collective
unrestricted egotism flares up; a struggle for existence intensifies;
might becomes right; and wars, bloody revolutions, crime, and
other forms of interhuman strife and bestiality explode on an
unprecedented scale. So it was in all great transitory periods
from one basic sociocultural order to another; and so it has
been in the present century. Notable disintegration of the sensate
order engendered the explosions of World Wars I and II, of a
legion of smaller wars, and of the bloodiest revolutions, revolts,
crime and violence in their worst forms. These explosions have
made this century the bloodiest of all the preceding twenty-five
centuries of Greco-Roman and Western history.

Wars, revolutions, revolts, and crimes have in their turn greatly hastened the disintegration of the sensate order. It continues
at the present time, becoming one of the three basic trends of
our age. Fortunately for all the societies which do not perish
in this sort of transition from one basic order to another, the
disintegration process often generates the emergence of mobilization of forces opposed to it. Weak and insignificant at the
beginning, these forces slowly grow and then start not only to
fight the disintegration but also to plan and then to build a
new sociocultural order which can meet more adequately the

gigantic challenge of the critical transition and of the post-transitory future. This process of emergence and growth of the forces planning and building the new order has also appeared and is slowly developing now. It is the third basic trend of our time.

The epochal struggle between the increasingly sterile and destructive forces of the dying sensate order and the creative forces of the emerging, integral, sociocultural order marks all areas of today's culture and social life, and deeply affects the way of life of every one of us.

The Epochal Struggle in Science

In science this double process has manifested itself: on the one hand, (*a*) by an increasing destructiveness of the morally irresponsible, sensate scientific achievements like the nuclear means of warfare invented and continuously perfected by the sensate scientists; on the other, (*b*) by an increasing number of scientists who refuse to cooperate in this destructive misuse of science and scientific creativity, in the establishment and growth of scientific organizations like our Society for Social Responsibility in Science, and, finally, in a transformation of the basic theories of science in a morally responsible, integral direction.

This change has already made today's science less materialistic, mechanistic, and deterministic—or less sensate—than it was during the preceding two centuries. For modern science, matter has become but a condensed form of energy which dematerializes into radiation. The material atom is already dissolved into more than thirty non-material "cryptic, arcane, perplexing, enigmatic, and inscrutable" elementary particles: the electron and the anti-electron, the proton and the anti-proton, the photon, the mesons, etc., or into the "image" of waves which turn into the wave of probability, waves of consciousness which our thought projects afar. These waves, like those associated with the propagation of light quanta need no substratum in order to propagate in space-time; they undulate neither in fluid, nor in solid, nor in gas. Around a bend of quantum mechanics and at the foot of the electron ladder, the basic notions of "materialistic and mechanistic science," such as matter, objective reality, time, space, causality, are no longer applicable, and the testimony of our senses largely loses its significance. The deterministic causality in the subatomic world is already replaced by Heisenberg's principles of uncertainty, by fanciful "quanta jumps," by a mere chance relationship or in psychosocial phenomena by "voluntaristic," "free-willing law of direction" or of immanent self-determination exempt from causality and chance. This last point is stressed by such leaders of the physical sciences as Max Planck, Albert Einstein, A. Eddington, E. Schrödinger, W. Heisenberg, H. Margenau, P. Dirac, and many others.

Similar transformations have taken place in the new, leading theories of the biological, psychological, and social sciences. In contrast to the superannuated, though still intoned, clichés of mechanistic, materialistic, and deterministic biology, psychology, and sociology, the rising significant theories in these disciplines clearly show that the phenomena of life, organism, personality, mind, and sociocultural processes are irreducible to, and cannot be understood as, purely materialistic, mechanistic, and sensory realities. According to these theories they have, besides their empirical aspect, far more important rational and even supersensory and superrational aspects. In these and other forms the most modern science has already become notably integral in comparison to what it was in the nineteenth century. This means an increasing replacement of the dying sensate elements of science by new integral ones.

The Integral Conception of The True and Total Reality

This replacement becomes clear if we look at a few basic problems in the physical, biological, and social sciences. We can begin with the problem of true and total reality. As mentioned before, sensate science of preceding centuries explicitly and implicitly tended to reduce reality either to matter or to that which is perceived by our sense organs. Such a science either denied or had an agnostic attitude toward any non-sensory reality. At the present time this conception of reality is already largely abandoned as narrow and inadequate by all sciences. It has already been superseded by an incomparably wider and more adequate conception of the total reality. Today this total reality is thought of as the infinite X of numberless qualities and quantities: spiritual and material, temporal and timeless, ever-changing and unchangeable, personal and super-personal, spatial and spaceless, one and many. In this sense it is conceived as the veritable *coincidentia oppositorum and mysterium tremendum et fascinosum*. It is the infinitude of infinitudes. In its totality it cannot be adequately described or denoted by words, concepts, definitions, signs, or symbols which have evolved to indicate, denote, describe, and define the finite, the limited, the specific differentiations or ripples on the infinite ocean of the total reality-value. They can define some of the ripples of this ocean but not the ocean itself; it contains all the ripples and at the same time is not identical with any nor with all of them. Even the most general categories of our thought, like substance, quantity, quality, relation, time, space, subject-object, cause-effect, being-becoming, are fit merely to identify the ripples but are inadequate to define the total cosmic reality-value. J. S. Erigena's "God Himself does not know what He is because God is not what" well expresses this inadequacy of our terms and notions for the definition of the total reality-value. It is not identical with what nor who, he, she nor it, matter nor spirit, subject nor object, nor with any of its differentiations; and at the same time it contains all of its known and unknown qualities. This explains why many a thinker called it "the Unutterable," "the Unexpressible," "the Divine Nothing" into which fade all things and differentiations (St. Thomas' *omnia exeunt in mysterium* of this reality).

On the other hand, being ourselves one of the important ripples in total reality, we can grasp roughly some of its important aspects. Of its innumerable modes of being, three forms appear to be essential: (*a*) empirical-sensory, (*b*) rational-mindful, and (*c*) superrational-supersensory. The new conception does not deny the sensory form of reality but makes it only one of its three main aspects. This new conception of the true reality, being incomparably richer and more adequate than that of the old one, is at the same time much nearer to the true and total reality of practically all great religions, especially of their mystical currents.

The Integral Theory of Cognition and Creativity

In accordance with this change, the scientific theory for cognition of the true reality has also changed. Though a few voices still intone John Locke's classical formula: *"Nihil esse in intellectu quod non fuerit prius in sensu"* (nothing is in our intellect that has not previously been in our sense) and monotonously repeat the old refrain that sensory perception and observation are the only ways to scientific cognition and knowledge, this theory of cognition has also become obsolete and has largely been replaced by a more adequate theory corresponding to the new conception of the total reality. According to this new integral theory of knowledge we have not one but at least three different channels of cognition: sensory, rational, and supersensory-superrational. The empirical aspect of the total reality is perceived by us through our sense organs and their extensions: microscopes, telescopes, etc. The rational aspect of reality is comprehended by us mainly through our reason: mathematical and logical thought in all its rational forms. Finally, the glimpses of the deepest superrational-supersensory forms of reality are given to us by true supersensory-superrational "intuition," or "divine inspiration," or "flash of enlightenment" of all creative geniuses: founders of great religions, sages, seers, and prophets, giants of philosophy and ethics, great scientists, artists, moral leaders, and other eminent creators in all fields of culture. These geniuses unanimously testify to the fact that their discoveries and creation of their masterpieces have been started by "the grace of intuition"—quite different from sensory perception or logico-mathematical reasoning—and then developed and tested in cooperation with the other two sensory and rational ways of cognition and creativity.

The Role of The Supraconscious in Discoveries and Creativity

Since the supraconscious mode of cognition and creativity is still questioned by sensate thinkers, who inexcusably confuse it with the unconscious or subconscious, it is advisable to outline briefly today's view of this problem. Very little is known of the supraconscious. What is known can be summed up as follows: (a) The supraconscious seems to be the fountainhead of the greatest achievements and discoveries in all fields of human creative activity: science, religion, philosophy, technology, ethics, law, the fine arts, economics, and politics. Without its genius and operation, through merely conscious and unconscious activities, only mediocre achievements are possible; never the greatest. A professor of English or of musical composition may know thoroughly all the rational rules and techniques involved in the composition of a literary or musical masterpiece; and yet, if he is devoid of the supraconscious genius, he can never become even a remote relative of the Shakespeares and Chaucers, the Bachs and Beethovens.

(b) The supraconscious creates and discovers through supraconscious intuition. It is different from all sensory intuitions (perception, observation) and from logical, mathematical, and syllogistic reasoning. (1) In contrast to senses and reason, intuitional inspiration or cognition comes as a momentary flash, different from a patient sensory observation or from mathematical, logical analysis. (2) The time moment and the circumstances of this flash can hardly be foreseen, predicted, or voluntarily produced. (3) The flash often occurs at the least expected moment and under the most unexpected conditions. This is true of nations and other organized groups as well as of individuals. The stream of their creativity in each and all fields ebbs and flows, rises and falls, shifts from one group to another, in an unpredictable and erratic manner. (4) The intuitional flash reveals the central or most essential nature of the intuited phenomenon, noumenon, or relationship of the new creative value. (5) The supraconscious intuition lies at the base of the whole sensory and logical knowledge or value experience. (6) The supraconscious is egoless: It transcends ego entirely and unconditionally. Dominated by the supraconscious, an individual becomes its egoless instrument, lifted far above the limitations of an ego. (7) The supraconscious with its creative intuition and other characteristics was noted long ago and called by different terms. The "self" (vs. "ego"), "atman," "purusha," the "Enlightenment," "Eternal reason," "Sublime stupidity," "no-knowledge," "divine madness," "nous," "grace of God," "divine or mystic revelation," "pneuma," *docta ignorantia,* "inner light" are the terms for it used by many thinkers and groups; "genius," "inspiration," "creative élan," the "sovereign intelligence which in a twinkle of an eye sees the truth of all things in contrast to vain knowledge," "celestial inspiration," and "supramental wisdom that goeth beyond all knowledge" are still other names.

Having outlined the essentials of the supraconscious, let us glance at the concrete evidence of its existence and operation.

The so-called "calculation boys" or "mathematical prodigies" present an example of an instantaneous operation of the supraconscious quite different from conscious mathematical calculation. These persons, often of low intelligence and consciously incapable of elementary mathematical reasoning or understanding, are able to make a complex mathematical calculation instantaneously, like determining the logarithm of any number of seven or eight digits, or finding intuitively "what factors would divide any large number, not a prime"; thus, given the number 17,861, they can say instantly that it is 337×53. When Arago in the presence of the French Academy asked Vito Mangiamele (ten years old and otherwise uneducated) the cubic root of 3,796,416, the child in about half a minute responded "156." Asked "What satisfies the condition that its cube plus five times its square is equal to 42 times itself increased by 40?" In less than a minute Vito responded that 5 satisfies the condition. And so on.

Among thirteen such prodigies we have two men (Ampère and Gauss) of eminent ability, and three who are rated good. The rest are of low or average intelligence. Some of these could not understand an elementary mathematical proposition or Euclidean theorem. It is also to be noted that the gift lasted only a few years with most of them, mainly in their youth. Whatever is the nature of this gift, one thing is certain: It is quite different from ordinary arithmetical calculation and cognition. Its operations are of the supraconscious kind, inexplicable and otherwise impossible.

In mathematical discoveries the role of supraconscious intuition has been enormous and indispensable. H. Poincaré, G. Birkhoff, Arago, and the whole Intuitional School of mathematics assert that "intuition and faith" serve as "the foundations for the rational superstructure erected by means of deductive and inductive reasoning," that they are "heuristically valuable," "of supreme importance," and "beyond reason."

Jacques Hadamard, himself a well-known mathematician, recently made a special study of the psychology of mathematical inventions. Among other sources, he used the answers to his questionnaire from eminent living mathematicians.

All these mathematicians state that their discoveries were "sudden and spontaneous," "without any time for thought, however brief." They report experiences resembling Gauss's. Gauss for many years fruitlessly struggled with a mathematical theorem. Finally, he reports:

I succeeded, not on account of my painful efforts, but by the grace of God. Like a sudden flash of lightning the riddle happened to be solved. I, myself, cannot say what was the conducting thread which connected what I previously knew with what made my success possible.

What is said of the role of the supraconscious intuition in mathematics still more certainly can be said of other natural sciences. Supraconscious intuition has been the beginning of most important discoveries in these sciences.

Sir Isaac Newton's discoveries of the mathematical method of fluxion, of the law of gravitation, and of the composition of light are classic examples of great discoveries that were started intuitionally.

The same is true of discoveries by Galileo, Haller, Black, Gauss, Ampère, Liebig, Humphreys, Faraday, E. H. Moore, Max Planck, Davy, Berthelot, Bertrand Russell, and others. In biology, the role of intuition was well stressed by C. Bernard. Eighty-three per cent of 232 natural scientists queried by the American Chemical Society admitted an unpredictable flash of insight which solved their problems with adequacy and finality.

It is not surprising, therefore, that a large number of great scientists—like Pascal, Kepler, Newton, Galileo, and others—were not only intuitionists, but mystics in the narrow sense of this term.

Philosophy also recognizes intuition. Beginning with the Upanishads in India and Taoism in China, passing through all the mystic philosophies of the East and the West; through Plato, Aristotle, the Neoplatonists (Plotinus, Porphyry, Proclus), the Neo-Pythagorians and Gnostics; St. Augustine and the Church Fathers; Pseudo-Dionysius, J. S. Erigena, Nicholas of Cusa; most of the great scholastics of the late Middle Ages (including St. Thomas Aquinas, especially in the last period of his life); up to the more modern philosophers—even such apparent rationalists as Descartes and Spinoza; such skeptical-critical philosophers as Hume and Kant, not to mention Schopenhauer, Fichte, Schelling,

Nietzsche, and such objective idealists as Hegel; and up to V. Solovyev, L. Tolstoi, H. Bergson, N. Lossky, W. James (in his later period), A. N. Whitehead, E. Husserl and other "phenomenologists"; N. Berdyaev, S. Kierkegaard, J. Maritain, and the Neo-Thomists; M. Scheler, K. Jaspers, M. Heidegger, and some of the other Existentialists—these and many other philosophers, practically an overwhelming majority, recognize some sort of intuitional axioms, "forms of mind," or intuitional truths as the basis of all the mathematical, logical, and sensory-observational verities in all fields of human cognition and creativity.

The supraconscious intuition plays perhaps a still more important role in initiation of technological inventions than in scientific discoveries. A detailed study of how inventors happen to conceive their inventions unmistakably shows the role of intuition; in most of these cases the first idea of the invention came like a flash, unexpected, often under peculiar conditions, and under other circumstances of intuitional insight.

"The veritable man of genius is he who acts by impulse . . . And genius is a grace." Thus J. de Maistre succinctly sums up the situation in his excellent criticism of Bacon's *Novum Organum.*

Still more decisive is the role of supraconscious intuitions in discoveries and creativity in language, the fine arts, the humanities, and the social sciences.

Language is an indispensable condition for human thought and creativity in many fields. Its invention and creation is one of the greatest marvels of humanity. Since it is a condition of rational thought, it could not be invented consciously and rationally. The creation of all natural languages was largely supraconscious.

Principal philosophies, main ethical systems, main codes of law, and basic humanistic and social science theories were formulated in their sublimest form long ago, when neither laboratories, nor statistics, nor rational techniques, nor the enormous body of empirical facts existed.

Only through the supraconscious could Plato have created his great philosophical system to which, A. N. Whitehead believes, the subsequent history of philosophy has been but a footnote. The same may be said of the place of the supraconscious in other great philosophical systems of the past, as well as in the great social science theories, in ethical and (to some extent) juridical codes. The most sublime ethical systems of the great religions were formulated long ago. All the intellectual ethical theories have not created anything equal to the norms of the Sermon on the Mount, or to the similar precepts of Taoism, Confucianism, the Upanishads, the Bhagavad-Gita, Yoga, Buddhism, Jainism, Judaism, or Mohammedanism. All the subsequent ethical theories and codes are but mere footnotes to these great ethical systems.

Nietzsche well describes this role of intuition or "inspiration." In the state of creative inspiration:

> . . . one becomes nothing but a medium for supermighty influences. That which happens can only be termed revelation; that is to say, that suddenly, with unutterable certainty and delicacy, something becomes visible and audible and shakes and rends one to the depth of one's being. One hears, one does not seek; one takes, one does not ask who it is that gives; like lightning a thought flashes out, of necessity, complete in form. . . . It is a rapture . . . a state of being entirely outside oneself. . . . Everything happens in the highest degree involuntarily, as in a storm of feeling, freedom, of power, of divinity.

Many great poets have similarly described the basic transmutation they experienced when "inspired" or possessed by the supraconscious.

And so also assert great music creators. "What, you ask, is my method in writing and elaborating my large and lumbering things?" writes Mozart. "I can, in fact, say nothing more about it than this: I do not know myself and can never find out. When

I am in a particularly good condition . . . then the thoughts come to me in a rush, and best of all. Whence and how, I do not know and cannot learn."

Beethoven states: "You will ask me where I get my ideas. I am not able to answer that question positively. . . . What we conquer for ourselves through art is from God, divine inspiration . . . Every genuine creation of art is independent, mightier than the artist himself, and through its manifestation, returns to the Divine. With man it has only this in common; that it bears testimony to the mediation of the Divine in him."

Beethoven clearly stresses the insufficiency of the rational mind for creativity. "Kings and Princes may be able to create professors and privy counselors . . . but they cannot create great men. . . ." "The new and original is born of itself without one's thinking of it."

In still greater detail Tchaikovsky describes this process:

Usually the seed of a future musical creation germinates instantaneously and most unexpectedly. If the seed appears at a favorable moment, the main difficulty is passed. The rest grows of itself . . . [A new idea gives Tchaikovsky a boundless joy . . .] One forgets everything, one is a madman . . . Sometimes inspiration takes flight, one has to seek it again—often in vain. Frequently one must rely here upon a quite cold, deliberate technical process of work. Perhaps such moments are responsible, in the works of the Great Masters, for those places where the organic coherence fails, and where one can trace artificial coherence, seams and patches. But this is unavoidable. If that spiritual condition of the artist called inspiration . . . should continue uninterrupted, the artist could not survive a single day . . . The strings would snap and the instrument would fly to pieces. One thing, however, is indispensable; the main idea of the piece, together with a general outline of the separate parts, must not be found through searching, but must simply appear as a result of that supernatural, incomprehensible and never-analyzed power called inspiration.

Similar statements are made by most great writers and poets. Schelling sums these up: "Just as the man of destiny does not execute what he wills or intends, but what he is obliged to execute through an incomprehensible fate under whose influence he stands, so the artist . . . seems to stand under the influence of a power which . . . compels him to declare or represent things which he himself does not completely see through, and whose import is infinite."

Finally, the role of the supraconscious is overwhelmingly decisive in religious and moral creativity. Lao-Tse, Zoroaster, Buddha, Moses and the Hebrew prophets, Mahavira, Christ, Mohammed—all the great moral teachers up to the more recent charismatic religious leaders—explicitly profess this role.

"I and the Father are one" (Jesus, John 10:30).

"Thou [God] art the doer thereof" (Jayminiya Upanishads).

"I live, yet no longer I, but Christ liveth in me" (St. Paul: Gal. 2:20).

"The works of a man who is led by the Holy Ghost are the works of the Holy Ghost rather than his own" (St. Thomas Aquinas).

"If any man is to come to God, he must be empty of all works and let God work alone" (John Tauler, *Following of Christ*, pp. 16, 17).

"Not me, but God working through me" (St. Theresa).

"It is Thou who wanted my debut and who took my essence in order to serve Thee as a symbol among men" (Al Hallaj).

The same idea stressed by mystics in their statement that the ego must die before one can attain union with God.

We see here the same transmutation of man into an instrument of the supraconscious which we saw in all fields of creativity. In religious and ethical fields this "becoming obsessed by the supraconscious" is especially conspicuous.

I have outlined the essentials of what we know about the supraconscious and its specific functions in truly great creativity and important cognition. Its main role seemingly is that of initiator and supreme guide to all notable discoveries, inventions, and masterpieces. In this capacity it cooperates with sensory and rational ways of knowing and creating, whose main functions seem to consist in developing and in testing the illuminating idea or pattern granted by the supraconscious intuition. This means that each great achievement or discovery is always the result of the unified work of all three—supraconscious, rational, and sensory—ways of cognition and creativity. This warns against acceptance of all sorts of false "intuitions" as supraconscious intuitions. As a matter of fact, the grace of this intuition in its full and pure form is visited only rarely upon the very few "select and annointed."

The truth of a creative masterpiece attained through integral use of all these channels is fuller and greater than that achieved only through the channels of either sensory perception, or of logicomathematical reasoning, or of intuition. The history of human knowledge is a cemetery filled with wrong empirical observations, false reasoning, and pseudo-intuition. In the integral use of these three methods, they supplement and check one another. Integral cognition means also that we learn about the total reality not only from empirical scientists and logical thinkers, but also from great religious and moral leaders like Buddha, Jesus, Confucius, Lao-Tse, and from the creators in fine arts, like Beethoven and Mozart, Homer and Shakespeare, Phidias and Michelangelo. They reveal to us, in Richard Wagner's words, *universalia ante rem.* So much for the integral conception of the total reality, cognition and creativity.

The Integral Theory of Human Personality

A similar struggle goes on between the old sensate and the new integral theory of human personality and human mind. The sensate theories viewed man mainly as an animal organism of the Homo sapiens species, and tended to interpret his nature and behavior predominantly in mechanistic, materialistic, reflexological, and other "physicalistic" terms. Some of these sensate theories have denied the reality of the human mind. Some others saw in it only two forms of mental energy: unconscious and conscious. The recent decadent form of sensate theories, exemplified by Freud's "notions," largely reduced the mind or human psyche to the unconscious sexual libido or id combined with sadistic Oedipus, Thanatos, and other complexes, with epiphenomenal "ego" and "super-ego" representing a modification of the same unconscious under the pressure of the family and society's "censorship." This sort of sensate theory of personality represents but a decadent and atrocious variety of the previous, sounder sensate conceptions of man. In Freudian and similar recent conjectures the distortion and degradation of human nature has sunk to its lowest level.

Fortunately, increased knowledge of human personality has led to an essential repudiation of these decadent sensate theories as phantasmagoric scientifically, ugly aesthetically, and demoralizing ethically, and to an emergence and growth of new, more scientific and adequate conceptions in this field. In these new theories man is conceived of as a marvelous integral being. He appears to be not only an animal organism but also a rational thinker and doer: in addition, he proves to be a super-sensory and superrational being, an active and important participant in the supreme creative forces of the cosmos. He is not only an unconscious and conscious creature, but especially a supraconscious master-creator capable of controlling and transcending his unconscious and conscious energies in the moments of his "divine inspiration," in the periods of his highest and most intense creativity. As mentioned previously, man's greatest discoveries and creative achievements have been largely due to man as the supraconsicous master-operator, assisted by man as a rational thinker and by man as an empirical observer and experimenter. If man were an organism motivated and guided only by libidinal or other forms of the unconscious, he would have had as little chance to become the highest creative agent in the known universe as have other biological species endowed only with the reflexological-instinctive unconscious and with the rudiments of a conscious mind. Specifically, the endowment of Homo sapiens with a developed rational mind and with supraconscious genius is responsible for his truly astounding and ever-growing creativity. As we see, this new integral theory of human personality again appears to be quite congenial to the religious idea of man as a son of God, created in the image of the Supreme Creator. This theory of personality is a more precise formulation of the triadic conceptions of man, prevalent in great religions. These conceptions viewed man as a creature having three forms of being: (*a*) the unconscious (reflexo-instinctive mechanism of body), (*b*) the conscious (rational mind), and (*c*) the supraconscious creator ("Nous," "Pneuma," "Spirit," "Soul," "Divine Self"). In the rational and the supraconscious properties of man lies the answer to the ancient question: "What is man, that thou art mindful of him?"

The Struggle for Existence vs. Creative, Unselfish Love

As a further example of the struggle between the decaying sensate and the emerging new integral theories and practices, we can take the problem of biological evolution of the species, of human behavior, and of mental, moral, and social progress of mankind. The sensate—biological, psychological, and sociological—theories of the nineteenth and of the twentieth centuries have viewed the egotistic struggle for existence as the main factor in evolution of the species and in human progress. The Freudian and other recent variations of these theories have considered sex and the hateful and destructive (sadistic and masochistic) instincts as the main factors of human behavior. Economics and other social disciplines have been based upon the postulate of egotistic man, motivated entirely by his selfish interests and relentlessly pursuing these objectives in all forms of deadly rivalry and milder competition.

These sensate beliefs are still reiterated daily in mottoes like: "It is rivalry and competition that made America great"; "The struggle for existence is the supreme law of life"; "For protection of our national interests all means of warfare, including nuclear ones, are perfectly just and right"; and so on.

These sensate beliefs have been unblushingly implemented and have resulted in the genocidal wars and revolutions of this century, with their mass-murders not only of millions of combatants, but also of noncombatants, including women, children, and old folk; into a wholesale destruction of cities and vastly populated regions; into the mad armament race and preparations for the next nuclear and bacteriological wars unrestrained by any laws—divine or human. In these and similar ways the partisans of these sensate theories, especially the governments of mighty nations, have openly declared themselves free from all restraints of international law and from all moral precepts of the great religious and ethical systems. In brief, during the last few decades sensate theories and practices have utterly degenerated and have led mankind to an extreme degree of ideological and practical demoralization which has been publicly approved by the governments and supported by a large portion of the Western and the Soviet blocs of nations.

Fortunately for all of us, during recent decades of the disintegration of sensate ideologies and practices, new—and quite different—theories and practices have emerged and have slowly grown in this field. The new theories have convincingly shown that the factor of mutual aid, cooperation and unselfish love has been at least as important an element of biological evolution as has been the struggle for existence; that the role of mutual aid and friendly cooperation has been incomparably greater in human progress than the role of inimical rivalry and violent coercion. These new theories have shown further that in his sound and creative behavior man is determined by sympathy, benevolence, and unselfish love as much as by egotistic motives, hate, and sadistic impulses; and that the energy of this love is indispensable for the generation, continuity, and growth of living forms, for the survival and multiplication of the species, and particularly for the survival and physical health of infants, and for their growth into mentally and morally sound citizens. Recent studies have disclosed also that altruistic persons live longer than egotistic ones; that love is a powerful antidote against criminal, morbid, and suicidal tendencies, hate, fear, and psychoneuroses; that it performs important cognitive and aesthetic functions; that it is the loftiest, most effective educational force for the enlightenment and moral ennoblement of humanity; that it is the heart of true freedom; that it can stop interindividual and intergroup conflicts and can turn inimical relationships into amicable ones. Finally, these studies have shown that a minimum of unselfish love is absolutely necessary for the continuing existence of any society, and that at the present catastrophic moment of human history an increased altruization of individuals and groups and extension of unselfish love in everyone for everyone are a necessary condition for the prevention of new wars and for the liberation of mankind from its gravest ills: bloody conflicts, crime, insanity, misery, and cussedness.*

If I were not restricted by space limitations I could also show that a similar drastic revision in many other basic theories of the psychosocial sciences has taken place over the last few decades: in the problems of methods of social research, of causality, of sociocultural structure and dynamics, of the total character of explanation and interpretation of politics and economics, ethics and law, fine arts and other cultural values. It is enough to say that in all these problems struggle between the decadent varieties of sensate and the newly emerging integral theories relentlessly goes on.

* Compare for details and evidence P. Sorokin, *The Way and Power of Love* (Boston: Beacon Press, 1954).

The Struggle in Philosophy

This struggle continues also in other areas of today's culture and social life. In the field of philosophy this double process has manifested itself: on the one hand, in a considerable diffusion of materialistic, mechanistic, and other sensate philosophies, fostered by Communist and Marxist governments; on the other hand, in a complete failure of all the officially supported efforts to create a modern, refined, and scientific system of materialistic and related philosophies. Despite all the financial and other help by the Communist and the Marxist governments to the contemporary leaders of materialistic and similar philosophies, no significant variation of these has been created; no new Democritus, Leucippus, nor Marx of dialectical or other forms of materialism has emerged. Instead a legion of Lilliputian popularizers has reiterated primitive and vulgar variations of the great materialistic philosophies of the past. If a few of today's materialistic thinkers have produced more refined interpretations of various cosmic, biological, and sociocultural phenomena, they have done so at the cost of an essential deviation from the orthodox principles of mechanistic, hylozoistic, and dialectical materialism in favor of either Hegelian dialectics or some monistic philosophy. This decline in the creativity of materialistic thought, in spite of its support by the Communist and Marxist rulers, is an eloquent testimony to the decay of sensate culture in the field of philosophy.

In a milder form a similar sterility has marked other sensate philosophies of recent times, such as: empiricism, positivism, utilitarianism, naturalism, physicalism, and realism. The modern variations of these philosophical systems have turned into the anemic, primitive, and poor relatives of these full-blooded and great systems of the past. Though quantitatively all these systems seem to be still dominant in the field of today's philosophy, their domination is rapidly fading due to the lack of creative genius in these currents of philosophical thought.

In contrast to this sterility, a much greater creativity is shown by the newly emerging systems of philosophy such as the Phenomenological, the Existential, the Intuitive, the neo-Mystic, the neo-Thomist, the neo-Vedantist, the neo-Taoist, the neo-Realist, the neo-Hegelian, and others. They all are different from materialistic philosophies and are more congenial to the integral theories of the total reality, of cognition, of human personality, and so on. If these philosophies cannot be regarded as a fully developed system of integral philosophy, they are its precursors and contributors. In the course of time these forerunners will produce a full-blooded, great system of integral philosophy in all its important variations.

The Struggle in Religion

In the realm of religion two trends have shown themselves in the simultaneous growth of: 1 (*a*) militant atheism and religious persecutions promoted by the Communist governments and some other groups, and (*b*) in a modest religious revival; 2 (*a*) in increased abuse and hypocritical misuse of Christianity and other great religions by the sensate ruling groups, vested interests, and ignorant fanatics, and (*b*) in spiritual purification and moral ennoblement of the traditional religions by those believers who do not distort their great messages and who practice what they preach, particularly the moral precepts of their faiths; and 3 (*a*) in the emergence of hate-laden, ignorant and odious pseudo-religious sects, and (*b*) in the new, intensely spiritual, profound, and truly altruistic religious movements.

The Struggle in the Ethical Field

In the ethical life of mankind continued decay of the sensate order has manifested itself in many forms. First, it has manifested itself in a progressive relativization and atomization of all the ethical values and legal norms. Sensate utilitarian and hedonistic ethics has declared all these values, precepts, and norms as mere human conventions which can be changed and even repudiated by everyone if they are found inconvenient, nonutilitarian, and painful for an individual or group. Second, the decay has manifested itself in an utter degradation of these values and norms to the level of mere "rationalizations," "derivations," and "beautiful screen" veiling the egotistic interests of individuals and collectivities, invented by a clever minority for exploitation of a stupid majority. In the sensate society of this century ethical values and legal norms have become mere rouge and powder to adorn an unattractive face of Marxian "economic interests," Paretian "residues," Freudian "libido," the psychologists' and sociologists' "complexes," "drives," and "prepotent reflexes." Third, as a result of this extreme atomization and degradation ethical values and legal norms have lost their moral prestige and binding power as effective factors of human conduct. Their "Thou shalt" and "Thou shalt not" have progressively grown null and void and like the Gospel's salt that lost its savor, they have become "good for nothing, but to be cast out, and to be trodden under the foot of man." Fourth, having lost their "savor" and efficacy, they opened the way for crude force as the only controlling power in human relationships. If neither religious nor ethical, nor juridical values control our conduct, what then remains? Nothing but naked force and fraud. Hence the contemporary moral cynicism, nihilism, and "might is right." Fifth, this state of extreme moral anarchy naturally has engendered extraordinary explosions of wars, revolutions, and merciless conflicts that have made this century the bloodiest in the twenty-five preceding centuries of Greco-Roman and Western history. This degradation and the atomization of moral values have also produced utter bestiality and inhumanity shown in these wars and bloody conflicts, and have increased criminality, and other phenemona of extreme demoralization. Finally, this anarchy has brought mankind to the brink of apocalyptic self-destruction in new world wars that threaten the survival of the whole of mankind.

Such are the principal manifestations of the progressively decaying sensate moral order.

Fortunately for man, this deadly trend is paralleled and increasingly opposed, first of all, by the trend of reestablishment and reaffirmation of the eternal, universal, and unconditionally binding basic moral values and norms. These values and norms are well formulated in the Sermon on the Mount as well as in the basic moral precepts of all great religions, ethical systems, and by all the great apostles of unselfish creative love. For the last few decades a notably increased knowledge of moral and legal phenomena has clearly shown the superficiality, inadequacy, errors, and poisonous effects of extremely relativistic, atomistic, utilitarian, and hedonistic sensate conceptions of these phenomena and values. Among other things this increased knowledge clearly established the fact that, along with changing and local mores, folkways, and legal norms are the basic moral values and norms of conduct which are universal, perennial, and obligatory for all societies and persons desiring a sound and good life. As a matter of fact, these eternal values and norms were found to be operating in all such societies of the past and the present. On the other hand, they were found to be lacking and inoperative in practically all groups that are in the state of utter demoralization, disintegration, and decay.

Besides this pregnant trend of reaffirmation of the perennial and universal moral values and precepts, the emerging integral order of ethics and law has manifested itself in the growth of moral heroism, sublime altruism, and ennobled moral conduct in an increasing number of individuals and groups; in the form of many organized movements for the abolition of war, bloody strife, misery, sickness, poverty, exploitation, and injustice; and in the form of social movements promoting the vital, mental, and moral improvement of man and his environment. Though sensate advertising and publicity pay little attention to these noble movements and actions; though sensate cynicists frequently even ridicule them by dubbing actions of moral heroism, sacrifice, and unselfish love "stupid sentimentality," or "utopian dreaming," or "impractical and unrealistic"; nevertheless, these movements and actions have been steadily growing in recent decades. Together with the reestablishment of perennial and universal moral principles, these actions and movements are the first harbingers of the coming spring of an integral moral order in a man-made cosmos.

The Struggle in Politics, Economics, and Social Life

The double process in the decay of sensate, and in the emergence of integral institutions and cultural values is going on also in political, economic, and social life. The decay of sensate political and social order proceeds in two ways: (a) in a degeneration of its free, contractual institutions, values, and ideologies into compulsory and fraudulent monsters born from contractual parents; and (b) in increasing depreciation and obsolescence of these parental institutions, values, and ideologies.

In order to grasp the full meaning of these statements one must keep in mind that all the diverse forms of human relationships easily fall into three main classes: (a) familistic, permeated by mutual love, devotion, and sacrifice; (b) free contractual agreements by the parties for their mutual advantage, devoid of love, hate, or coercion, but profitable for all contracting parties; and (c) compulsory relationships imposed by one party upon the other, contrary to his wishes and interests. Of these three relationships the familistic is the noblest, the compulsory is the worst, while the contractual occupies the intermediary position.*

The proportion of each of these relationships in the total net-

* See a developed analysis of these relationships in P. Sorokin, *Society, Culture and Personality,* quoted, ch. 5.

work of social relationships of each society varies from group to group and from period to period. For instance, the structure of social relationships in European medieval society from the eighth to the twelfth century was mainly familistic, compulsory, and only slightly contractual. From the sixteenth to the middle of the eighteenth century the proportion of compulsory relationships somewhat increased. In the nineteenth century the form of human relationships of Western societies became predominantly contractual.* This period was the golden age of Western contractualism. During this period Western society built a comfortable sensate edifice based upon convenant, contract, or free agreement for mutual advantage of its members. Its dominant capitalist system of economy was a contractual system of economic relationship between the parties involved, the employers, and the employees. This contractual (capitalist) economy was quite different from the coercive system of slavery and serfdom as well as from the system of relationships governing the members of a good family unified by mutual love, devotion, and sacrifice into one "we." In a capitalist economy each person is almost a free agent, freely choosing his occupation, freely accepting (or refusing) contractual agreement with his employer or employees.

In the political field the rise of contractual relations in the nineteenth century resulted in the elimination of autocratic, coercive governments and in their replacement by democratic political regimes, with the government contractually elected, contractually limited in its power, and bound to respect the inalienable rights of the citizen—his life, property, and pursuit of happiness, his liberties of speech, press, religion, association, choice of occupation, etc. The elective process became the main principle in recruiting rulers and public officials in states, municipalities, and associations. Contractual government of the people, for the people, and by the people largely replaced the

* See details on these changes in P. Sorokin, *Social and Cultural Dynamics*, *IV*, chs. 1-4.

autocratic government by the grace of God or by the violence and will of the rulers themselves.

Besides economic and political institutions, practically all other important organizations became contractual. Freedom of religion transformed the previously largely coercive religious affiliations and organizations into free contractual bodies: one was free to become, or not to become a member of any religious organization. A similar transformation occurred within the family. Marriage was declared a purely civil contract between free parties, in contradistinction to a compulsory marriage in which the parties were chosen, often against their wishes, by parents or other authorities. Becoming contractual in its establishment, marriage was also made contractual in its continuity and dissolution, in contrast to medieval marriage which was indissoluble in principle. Contractual liberties and inalienable rights of every person greatly expanded and permeated practically all organizations, even up to a contractual army of free volunteers in some Western countries.

Unfortunately, for several important reasons, not to be discussed here, at the beginning of the twentieth century, the whole sensate sociocultural order began to disintegrate, and with its decay the contractual fabric of Western society began to degenerate also into a less and less free, disguised compulsory fabric in the political, economic, and social institutions of the West. Since 1914 in many Euro-American nations the contractual form of government and capitalist economy have ceased to exist, while in many others they have been increasingly distorted by the intrusion of coercive or fraudulent simulacra of contractual governments and economic systems. Their place has been taken by various totalitarian forms of government and economy: Communist, Fascist, Nazi, military, oligarchic, and other varieties of Caesarism, militarism, and dictatorship.

In the contractual society of the nineteenth century, governments were elective and they controlled only a small fraction of the social relations and behavior of the citizens. Beginning with the economic relations of production, distribution, and consumption, and ending with the choice of occupations, amusements, residence, marriage, religion, education, political affiliation, ideological preferences, and so on, all these matters were freely decided by the citizens and private groups.

In contrast to this free society, in the completely or partially totalitarian nations of today the governments are self-appointed, not elected, nor contractual. If some of them still coerce their subjects to participate in so-called elections, these "elections" are but fraudulent mockery of real, free elections. And it is not the individuals nor private groups, but the government that now decides, controls, and regulates almost all the behavior, mentality, and relationships of the citizens in the autocratic nations of the Communist bloc, plus such countries as Turkey, Saudi Arabia, Formosa, Iran, Pakistan, Southern Korea, Thailand, and others. In so-called "democratic and free" countries, plus such nations as Spain, Portugal, several countries of the Middle East, and of Latin America, the governmental regimentation is more restricted, but it also grew far beyond its limits in the nineteenth century and is still expanding. A disguised machinatory-compulsory oligarchic regime has taken the place of the contractual regime of the nineteenth century. The compulsory regime largely consisting of self-appointed dictators and oligarchic cliques, has replaced government of the people, by the people, and for the people. The "free enterprise" of capitalist economy has totally or largely been supplanted by the governmentally managed and planned Communist, Fascist, Socialist, welfare-state and war-regimented economies.*

Similar degeneration has also occurred with many "democratic" values, procedures, and organizations. Free universal suffrage in election of governments and in decision of vital national problems has been either completely abolished or

* Compare P. Sorokin, *Crisis of Our Age* (New York: E. P. Dutton & Co., 1957), Ch. V.

greatly restricted, or replaced by its fraudulent simulacra. Its place has been taken either by violent seizure of power by revolutionaries, militarists, and various juntas, or by economic pressures, demagogic machinations, and monopolistic propaganda through plutocratically controlled press, radio, television, and other means of communication.

In other organizations, such as the family, degeneration has assumed the form of weakening its unity, stability, and sanctity. The trends of ever-increasing divorce, desertion, premarital and extramarital sex relations, childless marriages, growing infidelity and disloyalty, of decreasing mutual love, devotion, and responsibility of husband and wife, and of parents and children are the undisputable manifestations of this degeneration.

Free contractual labor unions have progressively turned either into compulsory government unions, or into semi-coercive political machines and "labor-racketeering gangs" autocratically manipulated by corrupt politicians and racketeers, imposing their power by fraud, threat, and violence upon a vast proportion of the laborers.

Finally, contractualism has degenerated shockingly in international relations. The triumph of contractualism in the nineteenth century led to contractual agreements between governments, to a development of international law, and to international arbitration courts like the Hague tribunal. These institutions effectively helped to prevent the explosions of wars and made the period from 1814 to 1914 one of the most peaceful centuries of Greco-Roman and Western history. In 1914 this peaceful order was abruptly terminated by World War I. Beginning with 1914, binding power of the international treatises and contracts has suddenly weakened, international law has been cast to the wind; all governments, without exception, have become double-crossers; violence and fraud in the form of devastating wars and destructive revolutions have been made the supreme arbiter of all international conflicts.

Besides this degeneration, sensate values and institutions have

also declined as manifest by their increasing uselessness, emptiness, and obsolescence.

Under the conditions of ethical atomism and potential nihilism, "contractualism tends to degenerate into a lawless, normless,
amoral, godless compulsion" or pseudo-contract under duress.
What is the use of the solemn declaration of equality of all
men or even of equal rights of all citizens to "life, liberty, and
the pursuit of happiness" when in real life there has grown up
the gigantic inequality of multimillionaires and hungry masses,
of powerful magnates and dependent "human dust" dominated
by all sorts of small and big bosses, beginning with a foreman
or ward-politician and ending with the political, economic, and
racketeering "big shots"? What is the cash-value of the freedom
of the press or other means of communication when press, radio,
and television are monopolistically controlled by a small group
of "the power élite"? The value of a free choice of occupation
or of the pursuit of happiness is also not great when millions
of the unemployed cannot find jobs and when millions are unhappy. In a similar manner, all contracts whose obligations are
broken by the parties concerned also become disserviceable,
as do the contracts of the members of criminal gangs, or of the
bosses of industry and finance, or of the members of a labor
union, profitable for these parties but detrimental to society
at large. All such contracts, freedoms, and equalities, with their
pompous slogans, become but the hollow, dead shells of the
great values they once embodied.

Similar decay through increasing emptiness has fallen also
upon the principle of universal suffrage as the method of election of government in the contractual society. If in its true
functions it has given "government of the people, by the people,
and for the people," now in its hollow form it gives instead only
"the government of politicians, by politicians, and for politicians." No wonder, therefore, that, in lieu of considering the
vote a great privilege as it is regarded by the citizens of the
true contractual society, voting is now viewed as a nuisance or

burden or "just a waste of time" by a large part of the voters. They prefer not to bother themselves with this nuisance and do not vote even in elections for high officials. The value of voting has depreciated so drastically that in a number of states citizens are forced to vote under penalty of law; failure to vote has been made a punishable crime. This fact alone testifies to the enormous deterioration of the elective principle. Once a great privilege it has become a burden imposed upon the citizens, punishable if neglected.

Similar degradation and obsolescence have happened with many political and social ideologies of the sensate sociocultural order at its previous creative stage. Whether they are the ideologies of Locke, Rousseau, Marx, or other varieties of "democratic," "liberal," "progressive," "conservative," "socialist," "syndicalist," "Communist," "anarchist" ideologies; or those of "equality," "freedom," "free enterprise," "planned economy," "welfare society," "of the new deal and the old deal"; all these ideologies which previously inspired with great enthusiasm millions of their adepts, at the present time are nearly dead; their "truths" are exposed as errors, their fire is gone, and their ashes are cold. As a result, at the present time most of the nations, their political leaders and ideologists, do not have any living, inspiring, nor creative ideology which successfully meets the challenge of our time and wisely points the safe road to the grand future. Instead all that they have is an atrocious concoction of tatters and odds and ends of obsolescent ideologies mixed up with their "home-made" ideological rock-n'-roll and jazz. If we are living in an age of general confusion, this confusion is particularly great in the field of political ideologies and values.

I have outlined the trend of decline in sensate political institutions, values, and ideologies. Let us now glance at a more hopeful trend, in the emergence of the seedlings of a new integral sociopolitical order.

This new sociopolitical order aims to be built upon contemporary scientific knowledge and the accumulated wisdom of humanity; it is animated not by "the struggle for existence and mutual rivalry," as the contractual, totalitarian, and oligarchic orders have largely been motivated, but by the spirit of universal friendship, sympathy, and unselfish love with the mutual aid that these attitudes imply.

So far there are only a few, and comparatively modest, manifestations of this new order. Let us briefly survey these new beginnings.

First, while the contractual order of the West has been crumbling and is being replaced by the coercive totalitarian regime, many Asian and African societies have passed from the hitherto dominant coercive order to the free contractual system of social and political organization.

Such transition has been experienced by the previously colonial nations, like India, Indonesia, Pakistan, Tunis, Morocco, and others, which regained their political and social independence from their colonial masters. In this way the regressive political change in the West is somewhat compensated for by the progressive political transformation of many Asian, African, and other societies.

Second, while the contractual order in international relations has largely crumbled, several new international institutions, like the defunct League of Nations and the existing United Nations, emerged in the attempt to build a world-wide contractual order instead of the previous "local" and "parochial" agreements by a few governments. Despite the many great defects of the United Nations and of other similar international institutions, they nevertheless contain great potentialities and can develop into important agencies of international peace for the unification of all the separate states into at least a loosely coordinated world-community.

The third and most important change consists of the fact that not everything is coercive and corrupt in the totalitarian and oligarchic regimes that supplanted the contractual order: Though the total fabric of these regimes consists largely of compulsory and fraudulent fibers, they contain, in addition, a considerable portion of the familistic filaments or relationships. For instance, though the total network of social relationships of the Soviet political and economic system is made up mainly of coercive fibers, it contains, in addition, a considerable portion of familistic and a small part of contractual fibrils. This means that the described degeneration in the contractual order of the nineteenth century into the totalitarian and oligarchic orders has not been totally regressive; parts of the previously contractual relationships have been transformed into much nobler familistic relationships. It is precisely these familistic relationships which are "the hidden power" that gives totalitarian systems their strength, moral prestige, and partial justification. Without the ennobling, unifying, and inspiring familistic relationships, the purely coercive part of the Soviet, the Chinese, and other "coercive-familistic" societies of our time would have crumbled long ago.

Along with the inhuman regimentation of millions of their citizens, the Soviet and similar regimes have liberated these millions from many forms of previous subjugation and exploitation. By their policies of "collectivization," "nationalization," and partial "equalization," these regimes have evoked in their citizens not only the mentality and behavior of regimented and enslaved prisoners, but also the ethos, the pathos, and the conduct of the free collective "we," spontaneously united into one vast family or brotherhood by mutual sympathy and responsibility, by mutual aid, free cooperation, and unselfish love.

Such a community is something quite different from "the lonely crowds" of today's contractual and oligarchic societies: In the familistic communities there are few, if any, "strangers," "lonely souls," "shut-ins," engrossed in their selfish ambitions and Lilliputian rivalries, or "free isolated individuals" who do not care for anybody and are not cared for by anyone.

It is this energy of unselfish love, in its crude or sublime varieties which animates, motivates, and empowers the familistic forms of human behavior, relationships, and social, political, and economic organizations.

This explains why a transformation of some contractual relationships into familistic ones and the growth of familistic flowers amid the horseweeds of totalitarian regimes and among the wilted and dried-up lawn-grass of democratic and oligarchic societies is of an epochal creative significance.

Fourth, familistic social institutions are proliferating not only in totalitarian but also in democratic nations in the forms of the "welfare and socialist states," "progressive republicanism," and "liberal democracy"; in the growth of various strictly familistic communities such as the Society of Brothers, the Hutteries, the Mennonites, the Friends' Communities; in the forms of more social service, cooperation, and mutual aid in an ever-increasing number of cities, towns, and villages; and in many other forms. All rapidly growing familistic relationships, communities, brotherhoods, and sociocultural institutions are indeed the forerunners of the new integral-sociocultural order. If fully developed, this order promises to be nobler and finer than the coercive and contractual orders of the past.

The emerging integral and familistic sociocultural order also implies several radical changes in the governments of the states, big business corporations, labor unions, and other powerful organizations.

Three significant trends in the qualifications of the new governments are already observable.

The first of these trends manifests itself in the rapidly increasing role of scientists and experts in the planning, developing, controlling, and executing of an ever-increasing part of the important governing activities and policies.

Many of the top-rulers of the existing governments, corporations, and labor unions are already largely figureheads rather than self-willed, energetic rulers. Their policies show that a notable part of them has become merely the executors of "the silent orders" of recent scientific discoveries and inventions. Before 1940 neither the Truman nor the Stalin administrations, neither Eisenhower nor Khrushchev, neither generals and admirals nor any of today's leading statesmen and politicians had the slightest idea of their "atomic," "hydrogenic," and "outer-space" policies which all the contemporary top-rulers are now carrying on. In this sense, today's ruling statesmen and politicians are increasingly becoming mere figurehead-executors of the "silent orders" of science and technology, conveyed to them by their scientific experts, advisers, and committees.

Such a trend portends the eventual withering of the hitherto existing governments of politicians, by politicians, and for politicians and their replacement by "governments of scientists and experts." Considering, however, the moral neutrality of today's science and scientists both of which serve constructive as well as destructive purposes, and the narrow competence of scientific experts, the good government of the near future needs, along with scientists, sages to perform successfully the task of integrating the narrow knowledge of each of the scientific administrators, and moral leaders to guide the governments in serving only good and not evil purposes. Without such guidance by sages and saints the government of scientific experts may turn out to be even more disastrous than the government of politicians.*

The foregoing considerations sufficiently explain why the ascending governments of scientists and experts need the efficacious guidance of their policies by the universal and eternal moral imperatives, and why future governments are likely to be the governments of scientists, sages, and saints instead of sensate governments of incompetent and often irresponsible politicians. Such are some of the trends of the emerging political order.

* See P. Sorokin and W. Lunden, *Power and Morality* (Boston: Porter Sargent, 1959), chs. 11, 12.

Three Basic Trends of our Time

Two Trends in the Fine Arts

The decay of the overripe sensate fine arts manifests itself in many ways. First, in decreasing creativity. The creative giants are all in the past, and today we seem to live in a world of artistic midgets. In music, Palestrina, Monteverdi, Bach, Mozart, Haydn, Handel, Purcell, Lully, Rameau, Couperin, Beethoven, and the like, all lived and created before or at the beginning of the nineteenth century. That century also had a galaxy of eminent creators in music, like Shubert, Schumann, Chopin, Berlioz, Wagner, Brahms, Tchiakovsky, Mussorgski and others: but even they were no longer of the stature of Bach, Mozart, or Beethoven. The twentieth century has hardly produced any master equal to the masters of the nineteenth century. Similarly in literature, the creative giants like Shakespeare, Goethe, Balzac, Hugo, Dickens, Tolstoi, Dostoevski, Melville, Twain, Whitman and the like belong to the pre-nineteenth and the nineteenth centuries; the greatest literary masters of the twentieth century, exemplified by the winners of the Nobel prize, are but midgets in comparison with these earlier masters.

The situation is similar in painting and sculpture, drama and other fine arts. "When there is no real fish, a crawfish is a fish," says a Russian proverb. We seem to have plenty big and small crawfish and hardly any real big fish.

Degradation of the fine arts and of beauty to the level of a mere means of sensual enjoyment—on a par with "wine, women, and song," a bottle of beer or a packet of popcorn or even to the level of a mere appendage of commercial advertising—is another symptom and consequence of the decadence of sensate art.

In ideational and integral art, and at the creative stage of sensate art, the value of beauty and art was regarded as a supreme end-value, indissolubly bound up with the other supreme values: God, truth, goodness, and the majesty of absolute beauty itself.

In contrast to this, nowadays art has become just a commodity manufactured primarily for the market, motivated mainly by *humanae laudis amore and temporalis praemii cupiditate* and aimed almost exclusively at utility, relaxation, amusement, the stimulation of jaded nerves or sexual excitation. Mass market demands cannot help being vulgar; therefore such an art cannot escape vulgarization. Instead of elevating the masses to its own level, it sinks to the level of the common herd. The extreme vulgarization of sensate pseudo-art is further evidence of its creative decline.

Hardly any record of a great musical masterpiece has been sold in as many millions of copies during the last decade as have records of the vulgar sham-music of "band-leaders" and "night-club" composers. None of the greatest singers of our time has become as popular or has amassed as great a fortune as have a legion of "the voiceless voices" whose singing is mainly a crooning, bleating, mewing, yelling, and "rock-n'-rolling." While people seem to read the great masterpieces of literature less and less, the sadistic and masochistic "pulp literature" of murder, insanity, and sex is sold by hundreds of millions of copies.

A further characteristic of sensate art in its decadence is its morbid concentration on pathological persons and events. From the realm of the Kingdom of God in ideational medieval art, Western art has descended, through the realm of the heroic, semidivine human society, to the world of normal human beings and finally, in our time, to the region of the social sewers with its abnormal and subhuman population consisting mainly of murderers, hypocrites, lunatics, sex maniacs and perverts, prostitutes, mistresses, cynical politicians, business Moguls, crazy teen-agers, hucksters of the arts and sciences, racketeers of religion, and other demoralized and desocialized human beasts. These animals make up the bulk of the personages and "heroes" of today's fine arts. They are centered mainly around criminals' hideouts, sex, insanity, and violence.

Typical again of the decadent phase of sensate art is the contemporary substitution of quantitative colossality for quality, of a "best-seller" for a classic, of technique for genius, of a short-lived, sensational "hit" for an immortal masterpiece.*

Side by side with this decay of sensate art we have the emergence of modern art and the first attempts at creation of the new integral forms of fine arts. The emergence and growth of modern art is significant as a manifestation of revolt against the "empty" sensate art and as a search for new and vital art. Modern art clearly departs from the shore of decadent sensate sham-art in quest for a new haven of beauty, but, with a few happy exceptions, the modern art-mariners are still in the midst of an uncharted ocean and have not yet arrived at the "promised land." In spite of this situation, their revolt against the semi-senile sensate art and their efforts of creation of new forms of art are the forerunners of, and contributors to, the emerging integral art. A few of these forerunners have already succeeded in creating imperfect works of integral Beauty, reunited with Truth and Goodness, value-laden and meaningful, beautifying the ugly, immortalizing the mortals, ennobling the ignoble, mentally enlightening, morally uplifting and spiritually inspiring.

3. THE REUNIFICATION OF TRUTH-GOODNESS-BEAUTY IN THE EMERGING INTEGRAL ORDER   Such, in a concise outline, are three great trends of our time. If they are adequately grasped, millions of singular events and changes incessantly occurring every day become comprehensible. Many of these changes can even be foreseen and predicted.

Among other things, this brief analysis shows that the new rising sociocultural order promises to give a spontaneous unification of religion, philosophy, science, ethics, and fine arts into one integrated system of the supreme values of Truth, Goodness, and Beauty. Such a unification signifies the end of divorce and conflict of science, religion, fine art, and ethics with each other— the divorce and conflict typical of the overripe sensate order.

* Compare Sorokin's *Dynamics*, quoted, I, chs. 5-13.

In the terms of Saint Simon's theory of the "critical" and "organic" periods in the life of great cultures, this unification means a new "organic" era in the history of mankind.

This struggle between the forces of the previously creative, but now largely outworn sensate order, and the emerging creative forces of a new integral order is proceeding relentlessly in all fields of social and cultural life, and in the inner life of every one of us. The final outcome of this epochal struggle will greatly depend upon whether mankind can avoid a new world war. If this apocalyptic catastrophe can be avoided, then the emerging creative forces will usher in a magnificent era of man's history.

CHAPTER TWO

Diagnosis and Prognosis of East-West Relationships

1. THE DECLINING SEPARATION OF WEST AND EAST   The classification of the human population, systems of culture, nations, and people as Eastern and Western is largely artificial and fictitious. At almost no time after 1492 have the peoples and cultures of Asia and Africa been absolutely isolated from those of Europe and the Americas, and their historical lives have hardly proceeded independently from each other. All that can be said on this subject is that for some three thousand years the contact and interaction of the peoples and cultures of Europe and the "Europeanized Americas" with those of Asia and Africa have been less intense and continuous, and their historical life less interdependent than those of the peoples living on the European and American or Afro-Asian continents. Even this relative separation from one another of the peoples and cultures of East and West has been steadily decreasing during the last five centuries, after the invasion of the Afro-Asian continents by the Euro-American "white man," following the development of means of communication and transportation.

At the present time this mutual isolation is greatly diminished, and if there is no new apocalyptic world war, the separation will certainly become less and less profound. Modern means of communication and transportation are daily bringing the West and the East closer and will continue to do so until these segments of mankind become as interdependent upon each other as are most of the peoples and ways of life of either East or West.

This trend raises a number of questions as to the coming mutual influences of the Euro-American and the Afro-Asian peoples upon each other. There is no doubt that these influences will be manifold and complex. In some cases Western values and institutions will replace Eastern ones; while in others, Eastern values and institutions may prevail over Western ones. For sometime in the future the resulting mixture of East-West cultural, social, and political features is bound to be eclectic, as it is for the most part at the present time. Eventually, if universal incineration and self-extermination of the human race do not occur, this "eclectic hash" may have some chance of being replaced by a cultural, social, and personal order composed of harmoniously unified elements of the great cultures of West and East.

Since in one short chapter it is impossible to deal with all these mutual East-West influences, I prefer to examine only one or two basic trends in the relationship of East and West, which are already under way at the present time and, in all probability, will continue into the future. The first of these trends consists of a progressive decline in the monopolistic creative leadership of the Euro-American peoples paralleled by an increasing participation in this leadership by the Afro-Asian peoples.

The second problem to be touched upon is an inquiry into what kind of integrated culture, social institutions, and way of life are likely to emerge in the future if the present eclectic mixture of West-East sociocultural congeries is to grow into a unified sociocultural and personal order in the human universe.

2. THE SHIFT OF CREATIVE LEADERSHIP   To reiterate what has been said about this trend in the preceding chapter, it can be generally stated that in creative leadership from prehistoric times up to the fourteenth century A.D., the peoples of Western Europe and the Americas seem to have lagged considerably behind those of Asia and Africa: (a) According to the prevalent

(largely conjectural) theory, the emergence of man as a deviant from the general anthropoid branch took place in either Africa or Asia rather than in Europe; (*b*) then, in progressing from the paleolithic to the neolithic, the Chalcolithic, the Bronze, and the Iron ages, the people of western Europe seems to have lagged behind those of Asia and Africa by several centuries, even by a thousand or more years; (*c*) in historical times, while the Euro-American peoples were still living under primitive sociocultural conditions, in Africa and Asia the great civilizations—the Egyptian, the Babylonian, the Sumerian, the Hittite, the Iranian, the Chinese, the Indus and the Indian, the Mediterranean (Greco-Roman and Arabic)—emerged, developed, and fluctuated in their blossoming and decline for centuries and millennia.

In brief, for millennia Euro-American peoples were "backward" in comparison with the leading peoples of Asia and Africa. The Western or Euro-American peoples were the last to assume the creative leadership of mankind. Roughly, only since the thirteenth century have they carried on "the torch of creativity," mainly in the fields of science, technology, fine arts, philosophy, economics, and politics. In these fields they have discharged their creative mission magnificently during the last five or six centuries. Their unprecedented and unrivaled scientific and technological achievements have made Europe and the Europeanized Americas the veritable center of human history during this period. They justifiably have made Euro-American civilization and people temporarily superior to the civilizations and peoples of Asia and Africa. These achievements have also permitted the Euro-American peoples to invade, to subjugate, and to exploit the Afro-Asian populations. The impact of Western scientific, technological, economic, and political civilizations upon the Afro-Asian cultures and peoples has been irresistible and overwhelming. It has evoked in the Afro-Asian peoples a strong desire and subsequent effort to adopt Western science and technology in order to eradicate or mitigate their misery, poverty, illiteracy, famine, and disease; to improve their ways of life; and eventually to liberate themselves from subjugation to the Euro-American powers. "It is the West that called forth the forces of resistance to its domination and endowed the subject peoples with the skills and institutions which could be most effectively used against herself. Western domination sowed the seeds of its own disintegration,"* so S. Radhakrishnan correctly sums up the situation. No less correctly, already in 1928, Charles Beard in *Whither Mankind* said: "If in due time, the East smashes the West on the battlefield, it will be because the East has completely taken over the technology of the West."

To a considerable extent this prophecy has already been realized. With the help of the Western nations the Eastern peoples have established their own schools, universities, scientific research institutions; have trained in Western countries their own scientists, technicians, political and business leaders; and are doing so increasingly. In Japan and Euro-Asian Russia they have progressed so far in this direction as to have almost reached the Western level of science and technology. Most other Eastern countries have not developed their scientific-technological culture as highly as have Japan and Russia, but they are rapidly closing the gap between their and the Western science-technology; and if no world war interferes, in the not too remote future they are likely to close this gap completely. In any case, these "backward" peoples have developed their scientific-technological culture to the extent of enabling them to regain their sociopolitical independence, to liquidate their colonial status, and "to kick out the white man" from his dominant position in their countries—including China, India, Indonesia, Burma, Egypt, and practically all the previous colonies of Europe and of North America.

All this indicates that the creative leadership of the West, which the Euro-American peoples have monopolized for the

* *East and West* (New York: Harpers, 1956), p. 108.

last five centuries, is about to end.* The Afro-Asian populations are now taking an increasingly active part and their share in this leadership seems to be rapidly growing. As a result, the creative center of human history, located for centuries in Europe and Europeanized America, is gradually ceasing to be confined within these boundaries. To a notable extent it has spread toward the East and is becoming "planetary" in the sense of being active not only in the West but also in the East.

From now on, the history of mankind will tend more and more to be staged on the scene of the Asian-African-European-American theater. From now on, in the great "plays" of history there will be not merely one Euro-American "star" but the several stars of India, China, Japan, Russia, Arabia, and other cultures and peoples. This epochal trend is already under way and is rapidly growing from day to day. It has manifested itself in the dissolution of the great European empires, in regained political independence for almost all colonial peoples of Asia and Africa, in the rapid growth of the political and social influence of these peoples in international politics, in the emergence of the potentially great Asian powers of India, China, Japan, and Euro-Asian Russia; in the decreasing political and cultural influence of Europe; in the accelerating scientific and technological development of Asian and African peoples; in the increasing number of important scientific discoveries and technological inventions made by Asian scientists and inventors (as concretely demonstrated by an increasing number of Nobel prize-winners among them) ; in the fading prestige of "the white man" throughout Afro-Asian continents; and in such symptomatic facts as the ever-increasing proportion of news, publications, conferences, lectures, and courses in Western schools which is being devoted to the events, cultures, and peoples of the East.

* On the termination of European leadership see E. Fisher, *Passing of the European Age* (Cambridge: Harvard University Press, 1942) ; P. A. Sorokin, *Social and Cultural Dynamics* (New York: Bedminster Press, 1962) , IV, 234ff.

In comparison with the little attention given these subjects in the West some sixty years ago, the place they occupy today is prominent indeed.

To these manifestations of the increasingly important role of the Afro-Asian peoples in the leadership of mankind is to be added a growing diffusion through the West of Eastern religious, philosophical, ethical, artistic, and cultural values. In these fields the West has seldom excelled the East. After all, Western Christianity—as the religious, ethical, legal, and even aesthetic foundation of Western culture from the fifth century to the eighteenth and, to a much lesser degree, up to the twentieth— was an Afro-Asian creation, born in Asia Minor and built from the Afro-Asian religious, philosophical, and ethical systems of Judaism, Zoroastrianism; particularly of the cults of Mithra and Mani, Cybele, Isis, and Osiris; and the religious and philosophical systems and practices of Hinduism, Buddhism, Taoism, Neo-Platonism, Neo-Pythagoreanism, and other Afro-Asian gnostic and mystic currents.* Through Christianity, and later through Mohammedanism, the East has influenced the West throughout the whole history of Western civilization and, to a lesser degree, continues to do so up to the present time.

In recent times Indian, Chinese, Japanese, and other Eastern philosophies, religions, and ethical, legal, and artistic values have begun to infiltrate the West, not only within the limited groups of academic, intellectual, and governmental circles but in much wider masses of the rank and file of the Western population. Hundreds of centers for various Oriental cults—Vedantist,

---

* On the sources of Judaism and Christianity see J. Breasted, *Dawn of Conscience*, New York, 1933; F. Cumont, *Les religions orientales dans le paganism romain*, Paris, 1929; *The Mysteries of Mithra*, Chicago, 1910; *After Life in Roman Paganism*, New Haven, 1922; S. Radhakrishnan, *East and West*, New York, 1956; A. H. Gardiner, *The Legacy of Egypt*, New York, 1947; S. Angus, *Mystery Religion and Christianity*, London, 1925; K. Lake, *The Beginnings of Christianity*, London, 1920-26 (3 vols) ; P. Gardner-Smith, *The Church of the Roman Empire*, Cambridge, 1932.

Judaism, as one of the main sources of Christianity, absorbed several Oriental religious, philosophical, and ethical currents of thought.

Bahaist, Mohammedan, Buddhist, Zen, Taoist, and others—have appeared and have been growing in practically all Western countries. In California alone there are at the present time several hundred such centers and cults. The techniques of various Yogis have been progressively popular with Western psychosocial scholars as well as with laymen and spiritual leaders. Important Oriental religious, philosophical, psychological, literary, and other works have been more often translated into the Western languages, carefully studied, written and discussed, and made accessible even to Western lay-readers. Comparatively recent Eastern sociopolitical movements and their methods, such as Gandhi's technique of nonviolent resistance, have been widely imitated and practiced by various sociopolitical movements of the West. Relatively recent Eastern religious, philosophical, and ethical systems like those of Swami Vivekananda, Ramakrishna, or Sri Aurobindo have been rapidly spreading and recruiting followers in America and Europe. The artistic styles of painting of China and Japan, of some Oriental architecture and, to a lesser degree, of literature, sculpture, and music have also been increasingly influencing Western fine arts. Some Eastern fashions of dress have also had their influence. Even several Japanese movies have received first prizes in international film competition.

In brief, the perennial influence which the East, through Christianity, had indirectly exerted on the West, has in recent times become a direct and easily recognizable influence.

There is little doubt that with a further development of means of communication and transportation this mutual interpenetration and mixture of East-West cultural values, ideas, institutions, patterns, and mores will continue to increase.

3. Possible Emergence of a New Integral Order in West and East   This trend of mutual interpenetration and combining of East-West sociocultural values and realities raises a momentous question: What is going to result from this trend?

Is the increasing mixture going to remain in the form of eclectic congeries of the elements of the Oriental-Occidental civilizations, or has it a fair chance to be integrated into a new, unified *Weltanschauung* and sociocultural order made up of the elements and values of both East and West?

Nobody, least of all myself, can give an infallible answer to this question. All that one can offer in regard to it is a guess which may or may not be correct. Just as a guess, I venture to outline my "prognostication" in this matter. This prognostication is based upon my general theory of sociocultural change and upon my diagnosis of the present state of Western (and partly Eastern) culture—the theory developed and documented in my *Social and Cultural Dynamics* and other works.*

In this essay there is not enough space to outline this theory nor to elucidate what I mean by sensate, ideational, and integral (idealistic) sociocultural orders. Suffice it to say that each of these orders is based upon, and articulates in all its parts, a major postulate concerning the nature of the true and total reality-value. Sensate order is based upon the premise that the true and total reality-value is sensory and that beyond it there is no reality and no value. The ideational premise asserts that the true and total reality-value is the supersensory-super-rational God (Tao, Nirvana, Brahman, "The Divine Nothing," and their equivalents) and His Kingdom. The integral order is built upon the postulate that the true and total reality-value is the manifold infinity, *mysterium tremendum et fascinosum,* the veritable *coincidentia oppositorum* which in its infinite plenitude cannot be perceived or adequately defined by the finite human mind. Being a reflective part of this reality, we can, however, cognize at least the three main forms of its being: the *sensory,* cognizable through our senses; the *rational,* comprehended by

* For a full development of my theories see *Social and Cultural Dynamics* (4 vols.) ; *Society, Culture and Personality; Man and Society in Calamity; The Reconstruction of Humanity; Crisis of Our Age.* These works have been published in several foreign translations.

our logical mathematical (rational) thought; and the *super-sensory-superrational,* intuited directly by the supersensory-super-rational human genius, especially by all the great creative dis-coverers in all fields of the sociocultural universe and, to a much more modest degree, occasionally, by ordinary human beings.

By limiting my explanatory remarks to these lines and assum-ing that there is not going to be an explosion of an apocalyptic-nuclear-bacteriological-chemical-world war (though in my opin-ion such a war now has about a fifty-fifty chance of occurring), I can state my prognostications in the form of the following hypotheses:

A. Since the sensate sociocultural order, dominant in the Western world for the last five centuries, is at the present time in a state of decay, it is bound to be replaced by a new, probably integral, sociocultural order—if the Western peoples are destined to continue their creative historical life. At the present time the first "spring blades" of this integral order are already emerging and slowly growing. The epochal struggle between the dying sensate and the emerging integral orders is paramount; it is the deepest and the greatest struggle of our time and of future decades. All the other conflicts—capitalism vs. communism, democracy vs. totalitarianism, religion vs. athe-ism or agnosticism, materialism vs. idealism, "freedom" vs. "com-pulsory regimentation," and other contemporary battle fronts—are but partial manifestations of this all-pervading, total and global struggle between the disintegrating sensate and the coming integral orders. This gigantic struggle is going on now in all aspects of social life and in all areas of Western culture—in science, philosophy, religion, ethics, law, fine arts, politics, and economics. It goes on within our souls, our minds, our bodies and our overt behavior.

B. Under the impact of the scientific and technological Western civilization, the traditional, largely ideational, socio-cultural order which was for a long time dominant in the Eastern countries of India, China, Tibet, Ceylon, Burma, Japan,

Indonesia, Arabia, and other countries, has also largely disintegrated and at the present time is clearly moribund. For this reason the Eastern peoples are confronted with the urgent task of creating and establishing a new sociocultural order. This new order is not likely to be either a modified form of their dying ideational order or an Eastern variety of the sensate order. The coming order is more likely to be an Eastern form of the integral order, similar in its basic traits to the emerging Western integral order but different from it in most of its secondary characteristics.

Now and for some time in the future one of the main differences between the emerging Western and Eastern integral orders is likely to be the following: The establishment of the Western integral order out of the hitherto dominant sensate order is possible only through (a) de-emphasis of material, physical realities and values occupying an unduly pre-eminent position in the sensate *Weltanschauung* and civilization, and (b) through supplementation of these reality-values by rational and supersensory ones, which are underdeveloped and undervalued in sensate cultures. The integral order as a unified system of the sensory, the rational, and the supersensory-superrational realities and values requires this deemphasis and supplementation. Without this internal reconstruction no integral order can be built from the remaining debris of the previously dominant but now moribund sensate order.

Unlike the situation in the West, the establishment of an Eastern integral order in place of the disintegrating ideational order is possible only through a greater emphasis and supplementation of the ideational realities and values by the noblest forms of the sensate and rational realities and values largely neglected and underdeveloped in the Eastern ideational sociocultural orders. The material standard of living of the Eastern peoples still remains so low, their poverty and physical misery is so appalling, and their basic biological needs are satisfied so poorly that no integral order can be built without a notable improvement in the material conditions of the Eastern masses of population.

In other words, to build up the new integral order the Eastern peoples in the near future will be focusing their efforts on the improvement of their material conditions along with the ennoblement and integral reconstruction of their rational and ideational values. To build an integral order, on the other hand, the Western peoples will increasingly "spiritualize" and "idealize" the Western world by: (*a*) abandoning sensate pseudo-realities; (*b*) by ennobling the perennial and universal sensate values; (*c*) by adding to these the rational and superrational-supersensory realities and values, and (*d*) by integrating all these forms of the reality-values into one unified integral system.

C. This means that, starting from almost opposite forms of sociocultural orders, the East and the West are confronting a basically similar task: that of building a new integral order in place of their respective crumbling ones. This does not mean that these integral orders would be identical in all respects. If realized, the order would certainly be built in "the Eastern style" in the East and in "the Western style" in the West—each style differing from the other in its secondary characteristics, in its concrete forms, colors, patterns, and other details.

D. If the suicidal third world war is avoided, the totality of existing sociocultural conditions is rather propitious for building the West-East varieties of the integral order. Its emergence and growth appear to be more probable than (*a*) either a continuation in a refreshed form of the disintegrating sensate order in the West and of the "petrified" ideational order in the East, or (*b*) the indefinitely long existence of an eclectic mixture of heterogeneous sociocultural odds and ends in the West, East and the whole human universe.

An indefinite continuation of the moribund sensate and ideational orders as the dominant cultural systems of the near future is improbable for several reasons. A recurrent history of the disintegration of previously dominant sociocultural orders shows that their decay is due mainly to the exhaustion of the limited fund of creative forces with which each order is potentially endowed. Like any empirical system, each sociocultural order has a limited fund of creative potentials; otherwise it would be an infinitely creative god inexhaustible in its creative forces. Having realized its limited creative potentials in its achievements, eventually each order is bound to exhaust its creative fund, to become sterile and incapable of meeting the urgent needs of its people or of society. Once it has become creatively sterile, the order cannot avoid the disintegration or mummification of its empty shell. And once this kind of disintegration or mummification has started, it usually proceeds to develop until the dying system loses its dominant position, becomes a minor order in the total culture of a given society, and is removed as a dominant order from the living stage of history to its museum. Among the many instances of this kind of disintegration-mummification of great sociocultural orders there is hardly a single case where this decay has been stopped and the moribund system has been revived to continue its domination for any length of time.

For these reasons it is hardly probable that the present dying sensate order in the West and the ideational order in the East can be revived and made serviceable to mankind in the near future.

Also improbable is the prospect of the West, East, and all human culture remaining indefinitely in the state of a vast, eclectic "dump" filled with heterogeneous odds and ends of sensate, ideational, integral, and other sociocultural congeries. The disintegration of any great sociocultural order into a permanent eclectic cultural "dump" means not only the end of the previous order but the end of the creativeness of the peoples who live by that order. It is eloquent evidence of the incapacity of such peoples to create a new, unified sociocultural order. Any great culture that ends its life by turning into this sort of permanent "dump" loses its individuality and becomes mere material, mere "civilizational manure and fertilizer," for other great civilizations or cultural systems. And any people, society, or nation which cannot create a new sociocultural order in place of the disintegrated one, ceases to be a leading "historical" people or nation and merely becomes "ethnographic human material" to be absorbed and used by other more creative societies or peoples.

If at present and in the near future, no new and great unified sociocultural order is established either in the East or in the West, or among the whole of mankind, this will mean the end of the creative mission of man on this planet, the degradation and regress of all "the historical peoples" to the level of the uncreative, "unhistorical," human hordes eventually doomed to perdition in one way or another; for man's constructive creativity has been and is the most important factor in the survival of the Homo sapiens species, of its elevation over all other species, and of its mastery over the inorganic, the organic, and the superorganic forces so necessary for the continuation of man's biological and sociocultural life in the past, present, and future.*

If contemporary man can avert the impending catastrophe of a new world war, the regression of either the West or the East or of the whole human race does not appear probable. Such a misfortune has befallen often in the past and can still occur now within a single society or with a few peoples but it can hardly happen to the entire Eastern or Western continents and still less to all of mankind. There are no convincing symptoms of a total loss of creativity by all contemporary peoples or by the whole human race. And there is a vast body of evidence that man's creativity is continuing and in fact in some fields, like science and technology, has reached heights never dreamed of before and is still soaring higher and higher.

* See my essay "The Factor of Creativity in Human History," *Sociologia Internationalis*, 1963, Heft I, 55-66; *Main Currents in Modern Thought*, May, June, 1962.

For these reasons, this prospect of the irretrievable disintegration of the total human culture into a perennial, eclectic "dump" and of all the "historical," creative peoples into uncreative human hordes doomed to perdition, cannot be accepted as probable.

Thus, if neither a resuscitation of the decaying sensate or ideational order, nor a disintegration of all human cultures into a universal and perennial eclectic wasteland appears to be probable, there seems to remain only one course for the creative history of mankind in the near future, namely, the emergence and development of a new integral order as the dominant order in the East and the West. Its basic premise is more adequate and less one-sided than the sensate or the ideational postulates. The integral premise embraces in itself both of these postulates and unifies them into one integrated whole (*Ganzheit*). The integral standpoint permits us to cognize not only the sensory or the superrational-supersensory forms of being of the true reality-value but all of its three main aspects: the sensory, through our senses; the rational, through our logico-mathematical thought; and the supersensory-superrational, through the intuition of genius* and, to a smaller degree, of ordinary human beings. Guiding these three channels of cognition and creativity into one three-dimensional channel, integralism unifies into one supreme cognitive-creative team, science, philosophy, religion, ethics, fine arts, and their specific ways of comprehension of the true reality-value (now separated from one another).

Through its wider, deeper, and more adequate *Weltanschauung* the integral standpoint also supplies more fertile ground for building upon its postulate a grander and nobler social, cultural, and personal order in the universe than the

* For discussion of the supersensory-superrational intuition as the highest source of creativity and cognition, and the total structure of the human psyche and personality, see P. Sorokin, *The Ways and Power of Love* (Boston: Beacon Press, 1954), chs. 5, 6, 7, 19.

other two premises do. Just as in the past the integral order of Greece of the fifth century B.C. and that of the European culture of the thirteenth century were the peak periods of the Greek and the late medieval European cultures, so now an emerging integral order is likely to be more magnificent, wiser, more just, and more beautiful in comparison to the preceding, now moribund, ideational, sensate and eclectic orders dominating East and West.

Finally, at present the East and the West each has all the necessary material and sociocultural background for building the new integral order. In the West purified Christianity, the rich garden of Western philosophy, with its grand empirical, rational (including the "critical" and skeptic) and mystic systems, its idealistic and materialistic ontologies, its great treasury of magnificent masterpieces of fine arts and literature, its heterogeneous systems and utilitarian, hedonistic, sublimely altruistic, and categorically normative ethics and law, and especially its superlative science and technology—all taken together—supply infinitely rich and excellent material for unifying and developing it into a magnificent Western integral order.

The East possesses the purified great religions of Taoism, Confucianism, Hinduism, Buddhism, Jainism, Judaism, and Mohammedanism; the truly grand Eastern philosophical systems beginning with the Upanishads, Taoism, and "six orthodox" philosophies of India and ending with the recent "integralist" philosophies of Sri Aurobindo and other Eastern thinkers; the great ethical systems of the East; an inexhaustible fund of the superlative achievements in the fine arts; unexcelled and unrivaled techniques of various yogis; extraordinary insights into the highest and therefore deepest* states of "self"; the wisdom of distinguishing the true knowledge (*jnana, prajna, vidya*) of the true reality from a superficial pseudo-knowledge of its appearances (*avidya*). All these, reinforced and enriched by the

---

* According to Kafka's happy expression: "the deepest in man is his highest."

rapidly increasing cultivation of Western science and technology, supplies the most excellent material for building a resplendent, new integral order in the East.* Mutual borrowing and cross-fertilization of their materials by the West and the East greatly help both parts of humanity in the construction of their integral orders.

E. The establishment of this order would lead not only to a greater knowledge of all three aspects of the true reality-value and to a greater mastery of man over the inorganic, the organic, and the superorganic forces and forms of being, but among other things to a mitigation of the existing mental, moral, and social anarchy, an increase of interindividual and intergroup harmonious relationships, and to a decrease of social antagonisms, bloody wars, revolts, and crime. The integral system of values would meet in the best possible way the search for values and peace of mind sought for in vain by contemporary humanity among the moribund sensate and mummified ideational values. In all these and in other respects, the establishment of the new integral order would solve most of today's great crises and would uplift the human race to new heights in its creative life-history.

F. As mentioned before, the first spring shoots of this order have already appeared, are growing, and are already engaging in a struggle with the dying orders. If there is no suicidal war, the victory of the new emerging order over its rivals is fairly certain.

G. If established in its fully developed form, this integral order, like Plato's ideal state, will also decline in due time after exhausting its creative funds.**

H. Such, with my repeated reservations, are my "prognostica-

* Compare my *Ways and Power of Love*, chs. 19, 20, 21; F. S. C. Northrop, *The Meeting of East and West*, New York, 1946; R. G. H. Siu, *The Tao of Science*, New York, 1957; Stcherbatsky, T. *Buddhist Logic*, 2 vols., Leningrad, 1932.

** *The Works of Plato*, Jowett translation (New York: The Dial Press), pp. 308ff.

tions" concerning the future relationships of the West and the East and the coming dominant order in both segments of humanity.

More than thirty years ago I ventured to make several detailed forecasts of important things to come.* These included predictions of future devastating wars, bloody revolutions, totalitarian regimes, gigantic destruction, misery, the unleashing in man of "the worst of the beasts." Despite severe criticism of my prognoses on the part of fellow scholars, almost all my prognostications have come to pass. I hope my present prognostications will be as "lucky and correct" as my previous ones.

* See these forecasts in my *Dynamics,* quoted, all four volumes; particularly Vol. III, Ch. 16 and Vol. IV, Ch. 17.

CHAPTER THREE

Mutual Convergence of the United States and the U. S. S. R. to the Mixed Sociocultural Type*

1. THREE PROGNOSES   Leaders of the West assure us that the future belongs to the capitalist ("free enterprise") type of society and culture. In contrast, leaders of the Communist nations confidently expect a Communist victory in the coming decades. Differing from both of these predictions I am inclined to think that if mankind avoids new world wars and can overcome today's grave emergencies, the dominant type of the emerging society and culture is likely to be neither capitalistic nor communistic, but a type *sui generis* which we can designate as an *integral type*. This type will be intermediary between the capitalist and Communist orders and ways of life. It is going to incorporate most of the positive values and to be free from the serious defects of each type. Moreover, the emerging integral order in its full development is not likely to be a mere eclectic mixture of the features of both types but a unified system of integral cultural values, social institutions, and of the integral type of personality essentially different from those of the capitalist and the Communist patterns. If mankind does not avoid new world wars and cannot mitigate today's grave emergencies, then its future becomes problematic and dark. Such in brief is my prognosis about the alternative future of mankind.

* There are German, Spanish and Russian (abbreviated) editions of this chapter.

Mutual Convergence

My main reasons for this prognosis are three: First, in their pure or extreme form, both the capitalist and the Communist orders are very defective and cannot meet the needs of a good, creative life for future mankind. Second, both orders are serviceable only under specific conditions for specific periods. In different conditions and periods both become disserviceable and therefore unneeded. Third, progressively both orders in the Western and the Soviet blocs of nations* for the last three decades have been increasingly losing their specific features and "borrowing" and incorporating in themselves each other's characteristics. In this sense, both types have been withering more and more and are becoming more and more similar to each other in their cultures, social institutions, systems of value, and ways of life. This means that both types, exemplified by the United States and Soviet Russia, have been increasingly converging to the intermediary type, different from communism and capitalism. This intermediary type, for the time being, represents an eclectic mixture of the characteristics of both orders. However, given the necessary time for its peaceful development,

* In this article I limit my analysis to the Euro-American continent concentrating on the changes for the last forty years in the United States and Soviet Russia. In regard to China, where the Communist system is still largely in 'its first, coercive phase, I simply can state that, if the Chinese Communist order is given the peaceful conditions for its free development, in due time it also will experience a transformation essentially similar to that of Soviet Russia. The first phase of any violent revolution, and especially of the Communist revolution, is always predominantly destructive, coercive, and inhumanly cruel. Eventually, if the revolution is not suppressed, it passes from this destructive into an increasingly constructive phase. The predominantly destructive phase of the Russian Revolution is already over and it has now entered into its constructive phase (unfortunately interrupted by World War II and greatly hindered in its progress by the subsequent cold and hot wars), while the Chinese revolution is still at the end of its destructive phase and is just entering its constructive stage of development. See on these phases in the development of practically all great revolutions P. Sorokin, *Sociology of Revolution* (Philadelphia, 1924) and in P. Sorokin, *Society, Culture and Personality* (New York, 1962) Ch. 31. A Spanish edition of this work is entitled *Sociedad, Cultura y Personalidad* (Madrid, 1960).

it eventually will grow into a unified integral social, cultural, and personal order in the human universe.

2. THE DECAY OF REAL CAPITALISM   In this chapter I am not going to discuss in detail the first two reasons of my prognosis. For my purposes it suffices to say that if capitalism were able to meet successfully the urgent needs of contemporary humanity, it would not have decayed as it has in the leading capitalist countries and would not have met an increasing resistance to its development in so-called "backward countries." Any country, and mankind in general, rarely, if ever, discards any important value, or institution—be it political, economic, or other—as long as this value or institution renders a real service in meeting the urgent needs of a given society. If, in our case, the capitalist sociocultural order is increasingly abandoned even in the previously capitalist nations and replaced by the Communist, the Socialist, the welfare state, the guided democracy, the Fascist, the Nazi, the "corporative," and other orders, this means that it has become increasingly unserviceable and obsolete. This conclusion becomes particularly evident in the cases of formerly capitalist countries like Germany, England, France, the United States, and most of the Western countries where the withering of capitalism had already begun at the end of the nineteenth century, was often initiated by the leaders of capitalism itself (especially by those who introduced "the corporation economy"), and has progressed from that time "naturally," immanently, gradually, without being overthrown by violent revolutions or by military coercion of foreign armies. At the present time, this withering of capitalism has already progressed so far that in all Euro-American countries, including the United States, the genuine, "full-blooded" capitalist or "free-enterprise" system of economy has become only a sector in the total economy of these countries and not always the major one. For the last few decades, especially since 1914, side by side with this "full-blooded" capitalist system, based upon "full-blooded" private

property, there emerged and have grown "the corporation-economy" and "the governmentally managed economy"—both essentially different from the capitalist system. And with some fluctuations, these two systems of economy have been replacing more and more the genuine capitalist economic order. To understand properly this last statement, one has to be reminded of the fact that "full-blooded," classical capitalism is based upon "full-blooded" private property, which means the right to possess, to use, to manage, and to dispose of the owned thing. In the governmentally managed economy, the officials are not the owners of the national property they control; the owner is the nation and the government is only the manager of the nation's property. Similarly, in the corporation economy the board of directors that manages it is not the owner of the total property of a big corporation; in some two-hundred of the biggest corporations in the United States, none of the directors owns even five per cent of the property of the corporation. The owners are tens and hundreds of thousands of holders of the shares of stocks of these corporations. An overwhelming majority of these owners neither manages nor disposes of the corporation's property. These functions are discharged by the board of directors of each corporation who, like the government officials, are not its owners. In the governmentally managed and the corporation economy we have a basic split of "full-blooded" property; those who own do not manage, those who manage do not own. This basic difference from the classical type of full ownership upon which the capitalist system was based makes the governmentally managed and the corporation economies fundamentally different from classical capitalism (with which—intentionally or not—the corporation economy is still mistakenly identified, especially by corporation bosses who speak of it as "free enterprise," or "the capitalist economy").

As in practically all Western countries in recent decades, governmentally managed and corporation economy have been systematically growing at the cost of "full-blooded" capitalism;

and as this capitalism is already a minor sector in the total economy of the United States and of several other Western countries, this fact clearly testifies to the decay of the true capitalist system, as pointed out above.

3. THE SOCIAL LAW OF FLUCTUATION OF TOTALITARIANISM AND FREEDOM   In a somewhat different way, the same can be said of the totalitarian-Communist system of economy. By it is meant the system of economy in which private property is abolished; the total economy of the country is "nationalized" and in its entirety is managed by the government. It is "centralized," "planned" economy in which the government decides all matters concerning the production, the distribution, the exchange, and the consumption of economic goods. The Communist system is a mere variety of this totalitarian system of economy.

Under different governmental regimes and different ideologies this system of economy emerged long ago and has occurred many times in human history: in several periods of Ancient Egypt, especially in the Ptolemaic period; in Ancient Sparta and Lipara; in Rome, especially after 301 A.D.; in some periods of the Byzantine Empire; in Ancient Peru; in several periods in China, India, and many other countries—to mention but a few outstanding cases. It was initiated and introduced by all sorts of governments and under all kinds of "beautifying," "rationalizing," and "sanctifying" ideologies; by the Egyptian pharaohs, the Roman and Byzantine emperors, the Incas of Peru, the Chinese or European autocratic kings, the host of military conquerors, the religious authorities like the Jesuits in America and many monarchist, republican, democratic, military, Socialist, and Communist governments. No less diverse have been the "ideologies" that justified, supported, rationalized, and beautified this totalitarian system of economy and government; all sorts of ideologies—religious, moral, political, utilitarian, "nationalistic," "economic," sociological," and others, beginning with the traditional Egyptian religious beliefs and cult of the Pharaoh as God and ending with the recent Communist, Socialist, Nazi, Fascist, Labor Party, Pentagon, welfare state, and many "dictatorial" ideologies—have performed this role.

This means that the Communist system of economy and ideology is only one of many varieties of the totalitarian systems of economy, ideology, and political regime. In diverse forms they have been predominant in the past and have frequently appeared in recent times.

The types of economies, governments, and ideologies of all countries are not something constant but continuously fluctuate between the poles of the totalitarian and the strictly free regimes of the *laissez passer, laissez faire* type with a minimum of government control of social life, relations, and behavior of the citizens. During a particular period the governmental control of the economic, political, and other sectors of social life of the citizens may increase and the respective systems of economy, government, and ideologies experience a totalitarian conversion (in various degrees) ; at another period in the same society the amount and severity of governmental regimentation may decrease and its economy, government, ideologies, and whole way of life undergo a process of detotalitarianization or reconversion toward a free economy, government, ideology, and way of life.

As a matter of fact today's sociology has even a generalized formula that satisfactorily accounts for the how, when, and why of these fluctuations. In a simplified form the formula runs as follows: Every time when in a given society there appears an important emergency in the form of war or threat of war, or great famine, or great economic depression, or devastating epidemic, or earthquake, or flood, or anarchy, unrest and revolution, or any other big emergency, the amount and severity of governmental regimentation invariably increase, and the society's economy, political regime, way of life, and ideologies experience a totalitarian conversion; and the greater the emergency the greater the totalitarian transformation. Conversely each time the important emergency of a society decreases, the amount and severity of its governmental regimentation begin to decrease and the society's economic, political, ideological, and cultural systems undergo a detotalitarian reconversion toward less regimented and freer ways of life; and the greater the decrease of the emergency, the greater the free reconversion. I can add to this that these fluctuations—or the totalitarian conversions and the detotalitarian reconversion to freedom—depend little upon the wishes of the governments involved and take place as regularly as do mercury fluctuations in thermometers in accordance with the factor of temperature.*

In the light of this "social uniformity" or "social law" it is comprehensible why governmental control of practically all areas of social life invariably increases with the outbreak of war or pestilence or earthquake or famine or social unrest or any other emergency. Among other things the uniformity accounts also for a regular and often very sharp totalitarian conversion of the "free, democratic" economy and government in times of war or other emergencies. Further on, the formula shows that various totalitarian transformations of the systems of economy, government, and ideologies are not something rare but on the contrary are quite frequent in the history of practically all nations.

Finally, this "social law" also explains my statement of why the Communist-totalitarian variety of economy, government, and the way of life cannot meet successfully the vital and creative needs of a good life, free from desperate emergencies, if tomorrow's mankind is destined to have such a good life. The Communist and other varieties of the totalitarian economy, government, and way of life are the children of emergency-

---

* Compare for a detailed formula of this uniformity and for the vast body of evidence supporting it P. Sorokin, *Social and Cultural Dynamics* (New York, 1962), Vol. 3, Ch. 7; abridged, one-volume edition of the *Dynamics*, chs. 29-30; P. Sorokin, *Man and Society in Calamity* (New York: E. P. Dutton & Co., 1942), Ch. 7.

parents. They are the dangerously strong "medicine" applied to counteract the desperate "emergency sickness." Under the conditions of this "sickness" they are sometimes (though not always) helpful in overcoming the "illness" and in recovering the normal "health" of the sick body-social. As soon as its health is improved, this "medicine" becomes unneeded, even harmful to the society. For this reason it is progressively abandoned and replaced by the "normal" regime of social, cultural, and personal life free from an excessive governmental regimentation and other totalitarian features. Hence, we have the detotalitarian reconversion that regularly takes place with the mitigation of emergency conditions, as indicated in the outlined "social law" or the "formula of the uniformity."

The conclusion of this analysis in regard to today's Communist, "the miltary" (Pentagon), "Nazi," "pseudo-democratic," and all sorts of other "dictatorial" varieties of the totalitarian order is as follows: If in the near future today's desperate emergencies (of cold and hot wars, of great social unrest, of extreme poverty in a large portion of mankind, of deadly radiation, of overpopulation, and others) are going to decline, the greater the recovery of mankind from these emergencies, the greater decline of totalitarianism is to be expected. If instead of a notable decline the great emergencies of our time are going to last or to increase for a long time, then the Communist and other varieties of totalitarianism are bound to grow for as long as the emergencies last or grow. Eventually the lasting emergencies with their totalitarian offsprings may lead to a fatal catastrophe of the human race and may terminate for a long time, if not forever, the creative history of Homo sapiens on this planet. Great lasting emergencies like a grave sickness increasingly undermine the healthy and creative vitality of the bodies-social; and, if not "cured" in time, they can harm it fatally beyond the point of recovery and eventually lead the gravely sick organisms of nations, or even of all mankind, to inglorious death or to the incurable chronic agony of "the uncreative life in death." If we assume that today's grave emergencies are going to be mitigated by "normal," "non-critical" ways and means, then all forms of contemporary totalitarianism are going to decline; if the emergencies are going to last or to increase, then the immediate future will bring victory to the Communist and other forms of totalitarianism. If, after their victory, their "dangerously strong medicine" does not cure the grave emergencies of our age, then chronic "life in death" looms as the destiny of the surviving, disillusioned and gravely sick, part of mankind.

4. MUTUAL CONVERGENCE OF THE UNITED STATES AND SOVIET RUSSIA   Nobody can predict with certainty which of these alternatives will take place in the future. If mankind can avoid the catastrophe of a world war, then other emergencies can be mitigated or eliminated to a great extent. In these conditions the eventual decline of all forms of totalitarianism appears to be probable. If the emergency of such a war cannot be abolished, then there is no chance to eliminate other emergencies. In these conditions the temporary triumph of various forms of totalitarianism is to be expected. So far the international policies of the governments of both blocs of nations have been unsuccessful in abolishing the threat of a new world war and in establishing lasting peace. And there is no guarantee these policies can abolish this emergency in the future. If our hopes in this matter were dependent entirely upon the policies of the existing governments, then the future of mankind would be dark and uncertain.

Fortunately for all of us, the course of human history is only partially dependent upon the policies of governments. In a much greater degree it is determined by the collective, anonymous forces of humanity—by the totality of actions and reactions of every human being, every human group, and, ultimately, of the whole of mankind. If the policies of governments contradict the course of history which these collective, anonymous forces consciously and unconsciously, in planned and unplanned, and in organized and unorganized forms endeavor to realize, then in due time such governmental policies are "cancelled" and replaced by the policies promoted by these collective forces. Under these conditions, often the governments themselves are "dismissed" and replaced—in an orderly or violent way—by governments that are willing and capable of realizing the demands of the collective forces of humanity or, if you prefer, of the forces of historical destiny or of guiding Providence.

The discordancy between the course of history required by the interests of mankind and the course of the governmental policies of the United States and Soviet Russia for the last forty years, and especially since the Armistice, gives a good example of this sort of historical situation. While the politicians of both countries have been feverishly carrying on the policies of mutual vituperation, enmity, cold and hot war; while they have been madly engaged in the armament race and in preparation for a suicidal world war; while both governments have been trying to discredit, to hurt and destroy each other by all means available; while for this purpose in their propaganda they have been extolling their own virtues and magnifying the vices of the other government and fantastically exaggerating the irreconcilability of the values and of the biological, social, and cultural differences between the two governments and the two nations; while the governments have been promoting this policy of war, the collective forces of both nations, of mankind, and of history have been engaged in a different kind of work and have been performing a task opposed to the policies of both governments, of their politicians, and of their "power-elites."

Instead of a magnification of the allegedly irreconcilable differences in the system of values, in social institutions, in culture and in the ways of life of both countries, these forces have been mitigating and decreasing these differences and making both countries more similar to each other in all these fields. Often silently but relentlessly, these collective forces have been progressively eliminating the irreconcilability of the values and the real interests of both nations and have been building a bridge for their peaceful coexistence and cooperation. Instead of separating both countries from each other, these forces have been converging them toward the intermediary type different from the pure capitalistic as well as from the extreme communistic type. Both countries have been increasingly borrowing and adopting the values, institutions, and cultural features of each other. This convergence has already progressed so far that at the present time both nations are much more similar to each other—socially, culturally, and in practical ways of life—than they were at the beginning of the Russian Revolution.*

The net result of this convergence is a progressive mitigation and elimination of practically all the justifiable reasons for continuing cold or hot wars, the mad armament race, and the policies of armed conflict. The convergence has already progressed so far that at the present time there is no justifiable reason for these policies and relationships between the two nations. If the belligerent policies continue and if they eventually result in a new world war, the only reasons for this sort of catastrophe will be the inexcusable stupidity, greediness, power-lust and poorly understood tribal interests of the governments, power-elites, and of "the brain-washed" masses of both countries. There is no certainty that these blind and irrational forces will not temporarily prevail in the future, but if such a

---

* One of the gross blunders committed daily by the belligerent politicians is their assumption that neither the USSR nor the U.S. has changed for the period of forty-six years since the beginning of the Russian Revolution in 1917. American politicians still talk about Russia in terms of the Russian Revolution of 1917-20 and Russian politicians talk about the United States as it was some forty or fifty years ago. If these politicians had studied the enormous changes which the United States or France or England had forty-six years after the beginning of the American, great French and Cromwellian revolutions, the politicians would have understood the big error they commit daily in their silly utterances. Their criticisms applicable to either of the two countries forty-six years ago is quite inapplicable to each of the nations, as it is today.

catastrophe occurs, its reasons or motives cannot be qualified as justifiable, rational, and excusable.

Now let us briefly document the trend of increasing similarity and mutual convergence of both countries toward a mixed intermediary type. We shall begin this survey with the cultural values whch are already identical in both countries and are free from any mutual conflict in their content or in their functions.

A. *Natural Sciences and Technology*

At the beginning of the Communist Revolution, the Soviet government wanted to create a program of specifically "proletarian" mathematics, physics, chemistry, technology, and biology rather than that of "the bourgeois" mathematical, natural, and technological sciences. After some three years of unsuccessful efforts to realize this objective, the silly project was completely abandoned and Russian science and technology resumed their interrupted development as a real science and technology whose validity and propositions are equally obligatory for Communists and anti-Communists, for proletarians and bourgeois. During the last thirty-five years, scientific and technological progress in Russia has been so rapid and great that at the present time Russian science and technology are as advanced as those of any country, including the United States. In some fields they are somewhat behind, in others somewhat more advanced than the science and technology of the West. But all in all, they have reached the development of science and technology in the most advanced countries of the West. And Russian science and technology in their principles, propositions, theories, and methods are the same as those of the rest of the world. There is no more silly talk about the "proletarian" and "the bourgeois" sciences and technologies. The scientists, engineers, and inventors of the West and of Russia speak the same scientific language, understand each other well, and when given a chance by their governments, wholeheartedly cooperate with one another in the development of scientific knowledge and technological progress. In summary there is in this field no conflict, no irreconcilable interests, and no essential difference between the two countries. Both nations are fairly similar in these fields and are at about the same level of development. Under normal conditions, without misuse and abuse of scientific and technological achievements by their governments and militarists, both countries would have mutual profit from their scientific discoveries and inventions. This means that science and technology as values do not give any basis, any reason, any justification for continuation of the belligerent policies for "the salvation of science and technology from destruction by the Russian (or the American) barbarians." The scientists of both countries are quite successfully taking good care of scientific and technological progress, especially if they are not hindered in their highly important research by governmental interference.

B. *The Social Sciences and Humanities*

Here again, at the beginning of the Russian Revolution the Communist government permitted only the Marx-Engels-Lenin interpretations of social phenomena along the line of dialectical materialism. All historical, sociological, psychological, economic, political, ethical, and other theories that contradicted or deviated from this line were prohibited, their authors were often persecuted, their works could not be published, and an enormous number of "counter-revolutionary books" published previously were taken from the libraries and destroyed. Though the doctrine of dialectical materialism still remains the official doctrine of the Soviet government, nevertheless today's situation in the field of psychosocial sciences is very different from that of the first years of the Communist regime. First, the Soviet government has published millions of copies of many classical works by pre-revolutionary scholars and social thinkers, such as the works of the great Russian historian, V. Kluchevsky, or the works of an eminent opponent of the Communist government, G. Plekhanov, the works of eminent social thinkers of Russia— Belinski, Herzen, Chernyshevski—and many other pre-revolutionary works and texts in the social and psychological sciences which have little to do with the official dogma of dialectical materialism. By the way, the biological, psychological, and neurological theories of a most outspoken opponent of the Communist regime, Ivan Pavlov, have now become the cornerstone of many biological, neurological, and psychological theories and practices of Soviet biopsychosocial science, education, and therapy. On the other hand, such materialistic theories as the pan-sexual theories of Freud are radically rejected by today's Soviet social, psychological, and humanistic disciplines. (See the sharpest criticism and rejection of Freud and of the diluted Freudian theories of E. Fromm, K. Horney, and F. Alexander by Ivan Pavlov and other Soviet scholars in *Voprosy Filosofii*, No. 12 (1959), pp. 44-48, and other issues of this journal for 1958-64.) Second, for the last two decades Russian scholars in these fields have published a large number of first-class works in history, psychology, psychiatry, ethics, and others psychosocial sciences which do not follow at all the line of the dialectical or any other materialism. These works have been published with the permission of the Soviet government by the governmental printing presses. Third, besides the works of the Russian scholars and thinkers, radically deviating from the official line of Marx's, Engels' and Lenin's ideologies, a large and rapidly increasing number of the non-Marxian and the nonmaterialistic historical, economic, psychological, psychiatric, political, ethical, juridical, and sociological works of foreign scholars have been translated and published in Soviet Russia during the last three decades. For example, my own works, formerly banned in Russia, in recent years have been permitted to be imported there in small quantities. Fourth, though the Soviet official sociology still remains the sociology of dialectical materialism, factually under this name the Soviet sociologists have been developing theories which in several aspects happen to be more idealistic than are many prevalent sociological theories of the West.* Carefully reading many publications of the Soviet sociologists, I find myself in essential agreement with several of their theories, principles, methods, and evaluation. Having always been highly critical in regard to the basic principles of all sorts of materialistic philosophy and sociology, in the Soviet sociology of today I find, under the cover of the official sociology of dialectical materialism, many a current of the "integral" or "idealistic" sociological thought.

It is true that most of the Soviet sociologists, psychologists, economists, and social scientists still quote in their works the Communist "theological" scripture of Marx, Engels, and Lenin. And for a superficial reader these scriptural quotations from the works of "the Communist apostles and church-fathers" may give the impression that nothing has changed in the Soviet psychosocial sciences since the beginning of the Russian Revolution. However, when Soviet scholars were asked why they indulged

* This fact manifested itself also at the Fourth Congress of the International Sociological Association at Stresa, Italy, in 1959, as well as in the published reports of the Soviet sociologists about this Congress and today's "bourgeois sociology" of the West. The Soviet sociologists find "the bourgeois sociology" of today neglecting the great sociological systems of the nineteenth century, dodging the basic social problems, studying instead the unimportant, narrow problems of the commercial interests of various business firms, serving in this way mainly as the handmaid of business corporations, devoid of basic values of truth, goodness, and beauty, morally and socially nihilistic and cynical and essentially materialistic, hedonistic, and utilitarian in the bulk of its research. This sort of criticism of "the bourgeois sociology," together with their own basic sociological, ethical, and philosophical principles, led many "a bourgeois sociologist" at this Congress to say that the Soviet sociology turned out to be more idealistic than are many sociologies of the West. Every sociologist who systematically follows the sociological work of the Soviet sociologists, not in their superficial mottoes but in their real content, must acknowledge the essential correctness of this impression about the idealistic currents in the formally materialistic Soviet sociology. See the reports of the Soviet sociologists about bourgeois sociology in the Soviet journals: *Voprosy Filosofii*, No. 12 (1959), pp. 72-86; also *Vestnik Istorii Mirivoi Kultury* for 1958, 1959, and 1960.

in these "theological" questions, their answer was: "Don't you sign all your letters with 'very sincerely' or 'very truly yours'? And do you really mean this in most of your letters? Don't these expressions mean a mere accepted routine? Our scriptural quotations mean just this sort of the 'very sincerely yours' and nothing more." This answer explains the real meaning of scriptural quotations by Soviet scholars.

Fifth, even Communist leaders like Khrushchev and others have publicly expressed their disagreement with the Marx-Engels-Lenin views on a number of important points, like the inevitability of armed conflict between the Communist and capitalist worlds, and in other theoretical and practical problems. This official deviation from orthodox Communist dogma is an additional symptom of the substantial change in the Soviet psychosocial sciences.

Sixth, in public and especially in private meetings, Soviet and Western scholars have already found, to a considerable extent, a common language for discussion of their scientific problems and for mutual understanding of one another. Finally, a particularly strong criticism by the Soviet scholars of "the bourgeois" social and psychological sciences for excessive relativization of all values, for moral nihilism, for rampant "physicalism," "extreme empiricism," and "positivism," and for a pursuit of mainly material-utilitarian interests manifests the same "hidden idealism" of the Soviet psychosocial thought. The following quotations illustrate this point. Criticizing the papers of the Western scholars given at the Fourth International Congress of Sociological Associations, they say that the paper of R. Aron was "scientifically and morally nihilistic"; that most of the papers on the Marriage and Family "intentionally refused to give an evaluation and especially the moral evaluation of the reported facts. . . . Their allegedly objective research completely fails to distinguish between the moral and amoral [forms of the family and marriage]. Their position of an absolute moral relativism practically annihilates the difference between the moral and amoral, the just and unjust, the good and bad, the true and false values and facts. . . ." This atomization of all values by the bourgeois sociologists, the sociologists of the U.S.S.R., Roumania, and Poland countered by the Marxist-Leninist conception of the family as inseparable from the basic principles of Communist ethics.* "Marxian materialism, differing from vulgar materialism, does not denigrate in the slightest degree the importance and significance of moral motives in the behavior of a person."**

These seven classes of evidential facts show convincingly the essential change in the Soviet psychosocial disciplines after some forty-five years of the Russian Revolution. Today these sciences are undoubtedly freer from the rigid dogma of Marxian materialism, are more "integral" or "idealistic" than they were at the beginning of the Communist Revolution; in several points they are more "integral" or "idealistic" than are many currents of the psychosocial sciences of the West. Additional evidence for these conclusions will now be given, dealing with the contemporary currents of philosophical thought in the United States and Russia.

If for the last forty-five years the psychosocial sciences of Russia experienced this change, many currents of the psychosocial thought in the United States (and the West) have moved rather in the opposite direction, in the form of the emergence and growth of Marxian, economic, physicalistic, cybernetic, behavioristic, reflexological, sexological, biological, and other forms of what can be styled as the varieties of materialistic interpretations of man, society, culture, and values in their structural and dynamic aspects.

---

* The new Communist ethics is defined as "the ethics of solidarity, of unselfish help and support in the struggle for the liberation of man from the burden of exploitation, and oppression." This ethics is opposite to that of bourgeois egoistic individualism. *Voprosy Filosofii*, No. 12 (1959), pp. 41-42.

** *Voprosy Filosofii*, No. 12 (1959), pp. 78-81; No. 8 (1963), pp. 13-36.

There is hardly any doubt that for the last few decades the Marxian, the Freudian, the behavioristic, the cybernetic, the mechanistic, the physicalistic, the naturalistic, the sexological (Kinsey's type), the reflexological, the biological, the economic, and several forms of the quantitative interpretations have successfully invaded the fields of American psychology, psychiatry, sociology, anthropology, history, economics, political science, theories of ethics, law, education, and other psychosocial disciplines. If one compares in each of these disciplines a dozen of the representative American texts from the beginning of this century to contemporary American texts, the comparison will clearly show the growth of these currents of psychosocial thought in the United States. Elsewhere I have shown that these currents have been growing in modern American psychosocial sciences.* And practically all of these currents in their theories, ideologies, and techniques are apparently materialistic in one way or another.

This does not mean that the psychosocial sciences in the United States are now predominantly materialistic. It means, however, that for the period considered the materialistic currents have been in ascendance here and that today's difference between the Soviet and the American psychosocial sciences is notably less than it was in 1917-25. These disciplines in both countries have been converging to an intermediate position different from that which they had at the beginning of the Communist Revolution.

C. *Philosophy*

Many Euro-American politicians, journalists, ministers, and professors denounce the materialistic philosophy of Soviet Russia and stress the unbridgeable contrast between it and the prevalent

---

* See P. Sorokin, *Fads and Foibles in Modern Sociology and Related Sciences* (Chicago, 1956), Spanish edition under the title *A Chaques y Manias de la Sociologia Moderna* (Madrid, 1957), French edition under the title *Tendances et deboires de la Sociologie Americaine* (Paris, 1959).

nonmaterialistic philosophies of the West. If this problem is considered superficially, without a serious analysis of the real character of the Soviet philosophy of dialectical materialism, this denunciation and overemphasis of the differences between Soviet and Euro-American philosophical thought would seem to be correct. If, however, we seriously study the meaning of today's Soviet dialectical materialism and the main currents of contemporary Western philosophical thought, these "correct" conclusions would appear to be notably incorrect. Yes, the official Soviet philosophy is still Marxist-Leninist dialectical materialism. But do its denunciators realize that today's Soviet proponents repeatedly warn not to mix it with all sorts of "vulgar materialism?" Do the critics know that even in Lenin's *Materialism and Empiriocriticism,* published fifty years ago, and especially in today's commentaries on the new edition of this work by Soviet philosophers, the very concept of matter is defined in such a way that if you replace "matter" in this definition by the Hegelian *"Geist,"* the definition would fit this *Geist* (or Spirit) about as well as that of *matter?* "Matter is a philosophical category for a designation of the objective reality given to man in his sensations and perception. This reality exists independently from and is copied, photographed, and reproduced by our sensations-perceptions."* Spontaneous, continuous motion or change is the inherent and inalienable property of this reality. "The World is eternally moving and self-developing matter." "Its higher form is represented by organic matter." "It contains the potentials of sensations, reflexes, and conscious thought which *are actualized* in its dialectic development."** In brief, Lenin's conception of matter differs little from Hegel's conception of the incessantly and dialectically self-developing objective *Geist* realizing itself in the dialectic process of the *Geist* "in itself,"

* Lenin, *Sobranie Sochineny,* Vol. 14, p. 117.
** Ibid., Vol. 14, p. 124. See also F. T. Archinzev, "Poniatie Materii," *Voprosy Filosofii,* No. 12, pp. 143ff.

"in its otherness," and "in itself and the otherness" (thesis, antithesis, and synthesis). Since Marx and Lenin adopted and accepted practically the whole framework of Hegel's philosophy, we must not be surprised at finding that the difference between the Hegelian philosophy of "the objective idealism" and the Marxist-Leninist philosophy of "dialectical materialism" is mainly terminological. Factually by different terms—*Geist* and *matter*—Hegel, Marx, and Lenin designate an essentially identical reality and ascribe to it almost identical properties and a dialectic process of self-realization. Viewed so, dialectic materialism does not appear to be so terrible, so different from, and so in contrast with the Hegelian and other varieties of objective idealism in Western philosophy.

In the comments of contemporary Soviet philosophers, "the hidden idealism" of dialectical materialism and its similarity to objective idealism come out still more clearly. Like objective idealism, dialectical materialism contends that matter, like the Hegelian *Geist,* exists as objective reality independent from any constructions of the human mind, that this reality is cognizable through our sensations, perceptions, and concepts; like St. Thomas Aquinas, these philosophers assert that the criterion for true knowledge of this reality is the adequacy of our ideas about it, with its objective properties (St. Thomas' *adequatio rei et intellectus*) ; moreover, our concepts are not merely nominal words devoid of any general knowledge but they are "real" and contain knowledge of the general properties of objective reality. In these important points, dialectical materialism turns out to be similar to the philosophical realism of Plato, St. Thomas Aquinas, Hegel, and to other varieties of the philosophy of objective idealism, and quite opposed to all forms of philosophical nominalism, including the "constructivist philosophies" of "as if" or *als ob,* of pragmatism, positivism, agnosticism, logical positivism, existentialism, sollipsism, excessive empiricism, skepticism, relativism, and other species of the predominantly "critical" (in Hume-Kantian sense), skeptical, agnostic, nominalistic, and "subjective" philosophies of the West.*

Furthermore, dialectical materialism of today openly admits the category of the *absolute* (standards of truth, goodness, beauty, and of other values) along with the category of the *relative* because to be meaningful these concepts demand each other and because, dialectically, "the category of the relative contains in itself potentially the category of the absolute. Being opposite to each other, at the same time these categories mutually permeate and mutually pass one into another." (In this sort of statement one can easily see the Hegelian "identity of the opposites," "negation is affirmation," and other characteristics of Hegelian dialectical idealism.)

Following rigidly the line of dialectical logic, some of the Soviet dialectical materialists now and then develop theories congenial to the philosophy of a real mysticism (St. Augustine-Erigena-Nicholas Cusanus type) in regard to the conception of the true reality as the *coincidentia oppositorum,* or to the philosophy of Thomism and Platonism in a number of important philosophical problems. These tendencies explain why in the works of the Soviet philosophers so much attention is paid to the intricate problems of the Hegelian philosophy (like that of "the negation of negation") or to the works of several contemporary (Belgian, French, and German) Catholic neo-Thomists. The outlined characteristics of Soviet dialectical materialism explain also its negative attitude toward agnostic, "critical," relativistic, "fictionistic" or "constructivistic" (of "as if," or *als ob* type), nominalistic, "vulgarly materialistic," "skeptical," "excessively empirisistic" philosophies of the West.

In summary, the dominant Soviet philosophy of dialectical materialism contains in itself a great deal of "the hidden idealistic strains." Despite its use of materialistic terminology, it is much nearer to the Plato-Aristotle-Erigena-St. Thomas Aquinas-

---

* Compare P. V. Tavanez, "Ob instinnosti poniatii," *Voprosy Filosofii,* No. 12 (1959), pp. 110ff.

Cusanus-Hegel philosophies of objective idealism than to all varieties of "vulgar materialism."* In many respects the Soviet philosophy is less materialistic, or more idealistic, than skepticism, agnosticism, excessive empiricism and relativism, pragmatism, logical positivism, instrumentalism, existentialism, constructivism, naturalism, and physicalism in contemporary Western philosophy. In the course of some forty-five years after the Russian Revolution these "idealistic strains" have been increasingly permeating the Soviet philosophy of dialectical materialism. For these reasons there is no solid ground to fear the disappearance of idealistic philosophy under the impact of dialectical materialism; and there is no justifiable reason at all for starting various crusades of extermination of "the atheistic and materialistic" Soviet philosophy. In its present form it is already more idealistic than are many of the crusaders' ideologies. Left to its own immanent development, the philosophical thought of Russia in the form of dialectical materialism and in that of the increasingly emerging nonmaterialistic philosophies has been moving and is likely to continue to move toward various forms of idealistic, "integral," and other varieties of philosophy.

If on the surface the official Soviet philosophy appears to be predominantly materialistic, then on the surface the "official American philosophy" seems to be overwhelmingly idealistic and anti-materialistic. Our politicians, chambers of commerce, many ministers, our popular press, radio and television indefatigably denounce "atheistic and materialistic" Soviets and all forms of materialistic philosophies and ideologies.

If, however, one studies this problem more seriously, this impression undergoes a substantial change. The chief disclosure of such a study is that materialistic philosophies and ideologies

---

* In 1962, 948 books in philosophy in the total of fifteen million copies were published. Among these, fourteen volumes of Hegel in 30,000 copies, six volumes of Kant, Aristotle, Spinoza, Hobbes, Hume, and of many other philosophers in 15,000 to 30,000 copies each. See the details in the articles of Kaltakhtchan, Petrov, Kursanov, and others in *Voprosy Filosofii*, 1963, No. 8, pp. 58-73.

occupy an important place among the total philosophies and ideologies of this country. First, among American professors of philosophy there are partisans of the dialectic-Marxian, and other forms of philosophical materialism. Second, the majority of American academic philosophers belong to schools of philosophy which can hardly be called idealistic, rationalist, or "integral." They contain many strains congenial to materialism rather than to the nonmaterialistic *Weltanschauung*. Instrumentalism, pragmatism, naturalism, physicalism (as an imitation of the philosophy of the natural sciences), several forms of empiricism and positivism, behaviorism, utilitarianism, agnosticism, skepticism, Freudanism and psychoanalysis (taken as a philosophical system), atheistic existentialism, cultic quantitativism, excessive relativism, and the social philosophies of economic, sexological, endocrinological, reflexological, instinctivist, and similar interpretations of man and the sociocultural world can serve as examples of this kind of philosophy permeated by materialistic, mechanistic, physicalistic, nominalistic, relativistic, and similar strains.

Third, in their vulgar form the materialistic ideologies, especially in their economic variety, are the favorite philosophies of many chambers of commerce, business corporations, politicians, journalists, professors, educators, and of many other groups—both "highbrow" and "lowbrow." In their public addresses they often profess their devotion to highly idealistic philosophies and values; in their daily business activities, speeches, and interpretations, they follow in fact the purposes, ideologies, and values of a materialistic, commercial, profit-motivated character contradictory to their high-falutin idealistic propaganda. In their "social and economic philosophies" they are possibly the most energetic propagandists of the vulgar economic and materialistic interpretations of man, human behavior, and sociocultural facts and values. Such ideologies are called by them "realistic" and "practical" in contrast to all idealistic philosophies which they derisively dub as "utopian," and "unrealistic."

Fourth, a large part of the rank and file of the American population are also imbued with a "practical materialism" in the form of an excessive pursuit of the material values of wealth, comfortable living, sensual pleasures, and the like.

These and other forms of materialism occupy quite a large place in American philosophical, social, economic, political, and ethical thought and behavior, in the American system of values and sociocultural life. For this reason, only complete idiots or unashamed hypocrites can claim that the American (or any other Western) nation is free from "materialistic contamination," is completely idealistic and saintly, and, as such, is entitled to carry on "the holy crusade" against the "atheistic materialism" of Soviet Russia or China.

Along with these materialistic currents, there is a vast fund of idealistic, rationalistic, "integral" and nonmaterialistic philosophies, values, forms of behavior, of cultural and social institutions, of private and public activities in American sociocultural life. In academic philosophy this fund is represented by several objective and subjective idealistic philosophies and by such currents of philosophical thought as critical realism, neo-Thomism, phenomenologism, intuitivism, neo-Vedantism, neo-Taoism, integralism, neo-Hegelianism, neo-Platonism, mysticism and other nonmaterialistic philosophies. In religious life, practically all orthodox theological philosophies—Christian, Hinduist, Buddhist, Judaic, Mohammedan, Taoist, and others—are idealistic. They represent the philosophies of the masses of the population. In social and cultural life, the idealistic and nonmaterialistic forces manifest themselves in thousands of forms beginning with a multitude of social movements and the acts of generosity on the largest scale, inspired by highly unselfish and idealistic motives, and ending with many social institutions and cultural values serving the noblest ideals of Truth, Goodness, and Beauty.

For the last few decades both the materialistic and the nonmaterialistic currents have seemingly been engaged in a relentless ideological, social and cultural struggle for domination on the American scene. Nobody can be sure which of the rivals has been gaining and which has been losing in this struggle. One result of it, namely, the curtailing of the extreme forms of each current and an increasing "reconciliation" of the valid components of each stream into some sort of "idealistic-materi-alistic" or "integral" philosophy, seems to have been occurring.

The net result of this survey is that in the field of philosophy the real difference between Soviet and American philosophies is much less than is usually thought. If all sorts of philosophies—the academic, the "official," the popular philosophies of the masses, the "practical" philosophies of daily life, the philosophies embodied in the social institutions, culture, social movements, system of values, and behavior of the people—are considered, nobody can pass a valid verdict as to which of the nations is more idealistic or materialistic. Insofar as the idealistic and non-materialistic currents are seemingly growing in Soviet Russia, even in its official philosophy of dialectical materialism, and insofar as the increasing "reconciliation" of these currents is occurring in the United States, both countries are seemingly converging to an intermediary—integral—philosophical position and are becoming more congenial to each other in this important field.

D. *Ethics and Criminal Law*

The professed ethical systems and the legal codes of law of both countries are at the present time essentially similar to each other.* The basic ethical precepts of both nations extol the principles of unselfish love, mutual aid, and other moral com-mandments given in the ethical codes of practically all great religions and moral systems. The main differences in this field can be summed up as follows: (1) the Soviet ethical system views these precepts as binding and obligatory (or as "categoric

* See P. M. Egides, "Marxian Ethics about the Meaning of Life," and L. N. Mitrokhin, "The Problem of Man in Marxian Interpretation," *Voprosy Filosofii,* 1963, No. 8, pp. 13-36.

imperatives") on the ground of their own value and of their necessity for the well-being of human beings, society, and mankind, and not because they are commanded by God or superhuman authorities. In the United States the binding power of these precepts is based still, to a considerable degree, upon the religious grounds of viewing them as the commandments of God. (2) Soviet ethics stresses somewhat more the absolute, universal, and perennial character of these precepts than does the secular ethics (in contrast to the absolutistic religious ethics) of the United States, especially in its utilitarian and hedonistic varieties: In these branches of ethics its values and precepts are regarded as merely useful human conventions which are relative and changeable according to circumstances. This relativization of the ethical values in these branches of American ethics is strongly criticized by Soviet ethical thinkers and is often styled as an excessive atomization of moral values, amounting sometimes to a complete moral nihilism and cynicism. (3) As for the problem of the extent to which precepts are not only preached but also practiced by the Russian and American peoples, this question cannot be answered definitely. The most probable answer is that for the most part there is no great difference between the nations: a part of their populations practices what it preaches; another part sometimes practices and sometimes does not; and, finally, in both nations there always is a minority which openly denies these precepts or professes them hypocritically without practicing them to any significant degree. There is no solid ground to claim that ethically one of these nations is saintly and the other is sinful.

Like the ethical systems, contemporary codes of criminal law in both countries are also essentially similar to one another. They prohibit (and punish) practically the same perpetration of crimes—like murder, treason, theft, larceny, rape, indecency, and so on—against persons, the state, property, good mores, and public safety. There are, of course, secondary differences in regard to some of the actions considered criminal in one code and non-criminal in the other and in regard to the severity of punishment and court-procedures, but these differences hardly exceed those which are present in the criminal codes of Western countries. Perhaps the most important difference between the criminality of the two countries is that, according to official crimes statistics, the occurrence of crimes in Russia is less frequent than that in the United States and respectively the rate of criminality in Russia is lower in most crimes (except the political crimes against the government and the state) than the rate in the United States.

In summary, if at the beginning of the Communist Revolution there were notable differences between the ethical and legal codes of the two nations, at the present time these differences have largely evaporated—mainly because of the changes in Soviet law and morality—in the course of some forty-five years after the Revolution. Both countries as well as all others can stand and urgently need a notable improvement in their moral climate and behavior, but such an improvement can take place only through a free effort by their populations and not through military coercion and warfare.

E. *Education*

At the present time, in this field, there are neither important conflicting values nor differences justifying any animosity by the two countries toward each other. In regard to increasing literacy (100 per cent), development of a school system and mass education, Soviet Russia has reached the level of education in the United States. The membership of the Russian Communist party likewise is now as well educated as the membership of the American ruling elite. In 1928 there were only 6,000 members with a university and high school education among the members of the Communist party. Now there are some 2,000,000 members with such education. In 1928 Russia had only 521,000 technicians and experts. Now there are some 6,400,000 technological experts. At the present time in Russia there are some 30,000,000 pupils in elementary and high schools, some 2,000,000 in technical schools, and some 2,200,000 in universities and colleges of Russia. The differences that remain are of the mutually complementary kind rather than of the incompatible sort. As a matter of fact each country has already borrowed several features from the educational system of the other. Perhaps the most important of the existing differences are two: namely, Russia seems to be paying greater attention to the education and integration of the character of the pupils (along with the development of their intellect) than that of the United States; and the Russian system of education cultivates more the "collectivistic or familistic" spirit and attitudes (without suppressing much the individuality of the pupils) while the United States educational system fosters more the spirit and attitudes of individualism (without turning it into a wholesale rampant egotism). Furthermore, selection and promotion of pupils in Russia to the status of university students seem to be more severe and based more upon the personal achievements than they are in the United States, where many college students are in a college or university just because "going to college" has become fashionable and because the American upper and middle classes "can afford" to send their children. The strict selection on the basis of the personal achievement by the pupils in Russia is accompanied with state stipends and fellowships granted to all capable students. This gives to the capable pupils of the Russian poorer classes as much, perhaps even a greater, opportunity to become university students and subsequently to occupy important upper and middle, professional, governmental, or "executive" positions. However, these and other differences in the educational systems of the two countries are secondary and temporary: Each country at the present time is carefully studying the system of education of the other country and does not hesitate either to adopt a valuable feature of the other or to remedy some defect of its own system in the light of the educational experience of the other nation. Factually, in this field the spirit of mutual cooperation, complementation, and healthy competition already prevails over the spirit of inimical incompatibility still fostered by a few shortsighted politicians and selfish "crusaders."

F. *Sports and Recreation*

Before the Revolution, the American varieties of sports—hockey, American type football, baseball, basketball, volleyball, golf, squash, and others—practically did not exist in Russia. Other forms of sport such as tennis, soccer, skiing, swimming, skating, and so on, were practiced only as a variety of personal, domestic exercise without any large regional, national, or international competitive interests. Before the Revolution professional sport played a small part in Russia; and in the field of international sports competition Russia played no part.

At the present time the situation is quite different. During some forty-five years since the Revolution all the varieties of American sport have spread widely in Russia. Sport now plays an important role, is intensely cultivated, has assumed in part a professional and competitive character, and has resulted among other things in the appearance of Russia on the scene of international sports, particularly at the Olympic games, where the victories of the Russian teams have made Russia second to none in this field. This means that in her segment of culture present-day Russia has become more nearly similar to the United States (and to other Western countries) than it was before the Revolution. On the other hand, somewhat surprised by the sport successes of Russia in international competition, the United States and other Western countries have redoubled their efforts in the development of their teams, in cleansing sports of various corrupt elements, and in freeing their national athletes from the excessive influence of various commercial motives. In brief, here again we notice the convergence of both countries for their mutual benefit and growth.

G. *Fine Arts*

At the beginning of the Communist Revolution the government tried to develop "proletarian fine arts." Accordingly it called the greatest poet of Russia, Pushkin, "a mouthpiece for the degenerated aristocracy," banned several works of Dostoevski, Tolstoi, and other Russian writers, prohibited also the performances of such musical masterpieces as the *March Slav* and the *1812 Overture* of Tchaikovsky, several operas of Rimski-Korsakov and Glinka, and in other ways tried to inhibit, suppress and depreciate many other achievements of Russian and foreign "bourgeois" fine arts. Completely failing in this silly enterprise, the Soviet government has abandoned and since the end of the 1920's has radically changed its fine arts policies. At the present time all the previous achievements of Russian literature, music, drama, painting, sculpture, and architecture are glorified more than ever before. Their creators are extolled as great geniuses. Their works are published in millions of copies, are reproduced, performed, and popularized by all available means of communication. The living writers, composers, painters, sculptors, and artists, along with scientists and scholars, have become—from the standpoint of their social prestige as well as their economic standard of living—the new Soviet aristocracy.

A similar change has taken place in regard to non-Russian fine arts and their creators. If before the Revolution Russia translated the literary masterpieces of the foreign classics possibly more than had any other country, now this tradition has been fully restored and even greatly exceeded. The following statistics of books published in 1956 in Soviet Russia give an accurate picture of the situation described. In 1956 in Russia 59,000 titles were published, and in total 1,107,000,000 copies, not counting magazines and periodicals. This is about five books per person, a number quantitatively greater than in any other country. Among all the books published in the field of literature, first place is occupied by books of the old Russian classics; second place by the works of foreign classical and eminent authors; the works of contemporary Soviet writers occupy last place.

The situation is similar in other fields of fine arts. Not only Russian art masterpieces and their creators are known and appreciated in Soviet Russia but also foreign masters and their creations. Homer, Sophocles, Dante, Shakespeare, and others in literature; Phidias, Praxiteles, Michelangelo in sculpture; Bach, Mozart, and Beethoven in music—are revered as much in Russia as in any other country.

As for the relationship of Russian-American fine arts, even before the Revolution there was a widespread interchange and cooperation between these countries, particularly in the fields of literature, music, and drama. Great Russian writers, like Dostoevski, Tolstoi, Turgenev, Chekhov, and others were well known in the United States and even profoundly influenced important American writers. The same is true of the Russian music of Mussorgski, Tchaikovsky, Rimski-Korsakov, Glinka, Rachmaninoff and other important Russian composers. Russian ballet and theatrical art, represented by the Moscow Art Theatre and others, likewise were highly appreciated by and even influenced American ballet and drama.

On the other hand, Mark Twain, Edgar Allan Poe, Walt Whitman, Jack London, and other Amercan writers were as well known and as popular in Russia as in the United States. Modern American architecture was likewise highly appreciated in Russia.

While this mainly fruitful cooperation was interrupted during the first few years of the Russian Revolution, it has now been fully resumed and grows rapidly. Besides the exchange of eminent artists, symphony orchestras, theatrical companies, ballets and dancers, the music of contemporary Soviet composers— Shostakovich, Khachaturian, Kabalevskii, Prokofiev, Khrennikov, Miaskovskii, Glière, and others—is quite at home in the United States just as the music of contemporary American composers— Harris, Piston, Gershwin, Copeland, Bernstein, Hansen, Block, and others—is at home in Russia. In literature the works of modern American writers, like Sinclair Lewis, Theodore Dreiser, Hemingway, Faulkner, Steinbeck, O'Neill, and others are translated and widely read in Russia while the works of recent Russian writers like Pasternak, Sholokhov, Leonov, Dudintsev, A. Tolstoi, and others are known to American readers.

With some modification the same can be said of other fine arts, particularly of American architecture and of the art of movies and television. Mutual fertilization of the American and the Soviet achievements in these arts goes on increasingly to the benefit of both countries. There is not the slightest ground for any animosity between the two nations in this regard.

H. *Religion*

In this field the values and interests of both countries are proclaimed to be particularly conflicting and irreconcilable by many a crusader for religion or for atheism. In this country we hear daily the denunciations of "the godless atheism" of the Soviets in the name of our God-believing and God-trusting nation. In Soviet Russia, likewise, voices still advocate, in the name of science, an invigoration of atheistic propaganda against all sorts of religious superstitions, ignorance, and exploitation of the masses by "the opiate of the people's mind." In the first few years of the Communist Revolution this sort of conflict of atheism versus religion existed, indeed to a great degree. During these years the Communist government carried on a most militant atheistic propaganda campaign against all religions; severely persecuted, disfranchised, imprisoned, and executed many thousands of bishops, priests, and believers; confiscated the property of religious organizations; turned churches and temples into Communist clubs and warehouses; prohibited public religious processions and instructions; in a word, it was engaged indeed in fanatical warfare against practically all religions and their members. The main target of this policy was the allegedly anti-Communist, "reactionary," and "counter-revolutionary" propaganda and political action of the religious hierarchies, leaders, and organizations.

For various reasons this persecution and anti-religious warfare of the Soviet government had greatly relented by the end of the 1920's, and with some minor fluctuations this trend has continued up to the present time. Today the total religious situation of Soviet Russia is notably different from what it was at the beginning of the Communist regime. The changes have been so many and so great that the irreconcilability and contrast between the allegedly atheistic Soviets and the allegedly religious United States and officially Christian West have largely evaporated.

In Soviet Russia religious—*qua* religious—persecution practically disappeared. Instead, the Constitution of the Soviets proclaimed religious freedom to be every individual's inalienable right. If now and then someone is persecuted for some crime or policy associated with religion, or if the policies of the Soviet government now and then conflict with the policies of the Vatican or other religious organizations, prosecutions and conflicting policies of this sort are due not so much to the religious intolerance of the Soviet government as to the anti-Soviet and sometimes even anti-Russian secular political activities of persons or policies of the Catholic Church and other religious denominations. (Unfortunately, the policies which are inimical to the Soviet regime and often to the Russian nation are still relentlessly pursued by several religious hierarchies and organizations.)

The autonomy of the Russian Orthodox Church, of the Protestant, Catholic, Mohammedan, Jewish, and other denominations in religious matters is legally and factually established. Even more, the main expenses of the Russian Orthodox Church and of its Patriarchy are paid by the Soviet state. It subsidizes a large part of the expenses of the administration of the Russian Orthodox Church, of manufacturing the objects of religious ritual and cult, of training the priests, of printing religious books and publications. The State also supports financially the material needs of the religious personnel, and so on.

Mutual Convergence

At the present time thousands of churches are open and functioning in Russia; there are at least ten divinity schools of the Russian Orthodox Church with 1,600 students training to be Russian Orthodox priests; some 20,000 parishes with 35,000 priests discharging their religious duties; some 650 monasteries with 5,000 monks and nuns; all in all, according to the available statistics, the Russian Orthodox Church now has some 50,000,000 members (about 20 per cent of the Russian population). The Protestant denominations have some 5,000,000 members. Of the Protestant denominations the Baptists have been especially fast-growing during the last two decades and have 5,400 houses of worship with about 600,000 members. There are more than 1,000 mosques and 1,240 Catholic churches. (Even in prerevolutionary Russia, Catholic membership was comparatively small. This was partly due to the unfortunate policies of the Vatican which has often been inimical to the vital interests of the Russian nation. Due to the same inimical policies of the Vatican toward the Soviet regime—and now and then toward the Russian nation— the membership of the Catholic Church has scarcely increased and still remains small in comparison to the Russian Orthodox and the Protestant denominations.)

These basic facts outline the religious situation in Russia at the present time. From a state of atheistic warfare against all religions at the beginning of the Revolution, the Soviet government and Russia have passed now to the state of a religious tolerance and freedom not very different from the situation in the Western countries, including the United States.*

* In this respect the evolution of the Russian Revolution is typical of most great revolutions. Beginning with the oldest recorded Egyptian revolution (in about 3000 B.C.) and ending with the Cromwellian Revolution in England and the Great French Revolution, most of the great revolutions carried on a militant persecution of the dominant religions at their first, destructive phase and subsequently replaced it by policies of tolerance and a sort of freedom at their constructive phase. Compare P. Sorokin, *Sociology of Revolution* and *Man and Society in Calamity.*

I foresee a number of heated objections to these conclusions. Isn't atheistic propaganda still favored and even subsidized in Russia by the Soviet government? Yes, it is possibly still favored and still subsidized by the Soviet, though much less than before. But doesn't the right of religious freedom also involve the right to be an atheist? If the Soviet government subsidizes the Russian Orthodox Church there is no violation of religious freedom while it also finds it advisable to support the "atheistic denomination" which, as we shall see, is quite a considerable denomination in all western countries. And don't the atheists of the West freely carry on their anti-religious propaganda and are not their activities subsidized from various sources, private and sometimes even public? So on this point there is no basic difference between Russia and the West, including the United States.

But, the objectors continue, is not the number of atheists in Russia immeasurably greater than in the Western countries? The answer to this question depends upon what we mean by "atheism." If it means a disbelief in the dogmas of some of the institutionalized religions, particularly disbelief in an anthropomorphic personal God, then such religions as early Buddhism and many forms of religious mysticism have to be considered as atheistic.*

If by atheism is meant a disbelief in the principal dogmas of the main Christian denominations, then it remains unknown whether in Russia or in the Western countries, including the

---

* Early Buddhism explicitly denied the existence of an anthropomorphic, personal deity, soul, and any substance whatsoever. The only realities, according to this Buddhism, are some twenty-six "dharmas" and their incessantly changing combinations. Many currents of mysticism also view the ultimate, total reality as the infinite manifold or ocean that contains in itself all its differentiations—personal and superpersonal, spiritual and material, unchangeable and ever-changing, and so on. The veritable *coincidentia oppositorum* in its infinity is undefinable and inexpressible by any words, concepts, and definitions. According to these mysticisms any institutionalized religious dogma expresses, at best, only some of the infinite "ripples" of this *mysterium tremendum et fascinosum*.

United States, the percentage of such "atheists" is higher in the total population. This problem has not been seriously studied. Of the few existing studies, the study of Professor J. Leuba (*The Belief in God and Immortality,* Boston, 1916), shows that about forty to sixty per cent of American professors and students do not believe in the immortality of the soul, the divine nature of Christ, the immaculate conception of Jesus, or in several other dogmas of the Christian religions. A recent extensive poll of the population in various European countries by the International Research Associates disclosed that in Italy only fifty-one per cent believes in these dogmas, in Norway only forty-two per cent, in Belgium only thirty-three per cent, in France only thirty per cent; all in all, for Europe about seventy per cent of its polled samples of the population declared themselves agnostics and disbelievers in these dogmas. If these results are representative of Europe and the United States, there is no great difference between Russia and the Western countries in this respect.

If by true religiosity is meant, first, "the feeling of presence" (in terms of an eminent mystic, Brother Lawrence), that beyond the empirical reality of our senses there are other and higher forms of reality; and second, the practice of the moral commandments of Confucianism, or Taoism, or Hinduism, or Buddhism, or Judaism, or Jainism, or Christianity, or Mohammedanism (all basic moral precepts of these and other religions are essentially similar), then we do not have any even remotely adequate evidence for the claim as to whether the Russian or the American or the European population is more religious. Judging on the basis of various fragmentary data, I suspect that on this matter there is no great difference between today's Soviet Russia and the Euro-American countries.

The result of this analysis is that in the field of religion there certainly has been occurring a mutual convergence of Russia and the Western countries. In comparison with the early years of

the Communist Revolution, the religious conflicts and differences at the present time are immeasurably less significant and
important.

I. *The Marriage and Family*

In the early years of the Revolution, the Communist government intentionally tried to destroy monogamous marriage and
the family as the cornerstone of private property and the capitalist system. Complete legal and factual liberty of sex in its premarital and extramarital forms was proclaimed, together with
complete liberty of marriage, divorce, abortion, and other con-
comitants of the "glass of water" policy in sex matters, according
to which sex was compared with thirst which could and should
be satisfied from any glass available.

The disastrous consequences of this policy forced the Soviet
government, by the end of the 1920's, to change radically by
increasing drastic limitations of this sex-freedom. Instead of
glorification of unlimited sexual freedom, the Soviet government
began to glorify virginity, chastity, and fidelity in marriage, and
began to issue a series of decrees legally approving, sanctioning,
and requiring these virtues. To make a long and painful story
short, at the present time Soviet Russia has a more stable, more
monogamous and more Victorian attitude toward the family and
marriage than has practically any Western country, and especially
the United States. Divorce is not prohibited legally, but its
procurement is so heavily inhibited by financial and legal difficulties that it is practically impossible for an overwhelming
majority of the Russian population. Abortions are prohibited
and punishable. Premarital and extramarital sex relations are
strongly disapproved. So also are all ideologies, publications,
pictures, plays, novels, radio and television programs advocating
and glorifying sex-anarchy and sex-freedom. In general, sex and
preoccupation with sex now play a much less important role
in the social and cultural life of Russia than in that of the
United States and European countries. (See P. Sorokin, *The*

American Sex Revolution, Boston, 1956. There are Swedish, Japanese, Spanish, Indian, and Portuguese editions of this book.)

In summary, at the beginning of the Revolution the Soviet government and part of the Russian population could be accused of undermining monogamous marriage and family life and of promoting sexual anarchy and licentiousness. At the present time these accusations have been reversed: Soviet Russia is now stressing the excessive sex-obsession, sex-perversion, sex-anarchy, sex-abuse for commercial purposes, indeed the permeation by sex of the whole social, cultural, and personal life of the Western countries and the resulting disintegration of monogamous marriage and family life. In all frankness, Russia is more entitled to make these moral censures than are the Western countries in regard to Russia. Considering, however, that the modern sex-anarchy has never been approved by Western religious, moral, and public opinion; that the stable monogamous marriage and family are still sanctioned and desired; and that in recent times in the United States and in Europe a strong public movement for the stabilization of marriage and the family and for a limitation of the sex-anarchy has emerged and is growing; considering these Western trends and the tragic cycle with the "happy ending" passed by Russia in this field, these basic facts show again that in this segment of sociocultural life both countries have been converging toward a similar order of sex-life, marriage and the family.

J. *The Economic System*

In the introductory sections of this chapter it has already been shown that the real difference between the economic systems of both countries is much less than it appears to be on the surface and that both countries have been converging to a mixed type of economy representing the coexistence of (*a*) full-fledged free enterprise based upon private property, (*b*) of corporation economy, and (*c*) of economy managed by the government.

In the total economy of both countries the area of full-fledged free enterprise is already a minor area. In Russia it exists and functions mainly in regard to consumer goods, including such goods as accumulated savings, as ownership of apartment, automobile, or house, of a small piece of land or a small business managed by the owner, or of the tools of artisans, artists, scientists, and the like. All such goods are owned in Russia and can be disposed of or willed by the owner to his heirs in about the same way as they are owned, used, disposed of, and willed in the United States. In the United States this sector of the economy is larger than in Soviet Russia. Besides consumer goods it covers a large part of "small businesses" and of agriculture. In these last two fields, however, the economy of real free enterprise has unfortunately been shrinking for the last few decades, and this shrinking has continued up to the present time. In Soviet Russia, on the contrary, this sector has been somewhat expanding during the last two decades, particularly in the field of agriculture. The rights of the collective farms and of their members have been expanding especially since the decree of February 17, 1935, on the *Standard Rules of an Artel*. The land, cultivated by a collective farm, remains at its disposal forever. Each collective farm manages its own affairs autonomously. Each member possesses his own "private property"— a dwelling, a plot of land for his personal use, from ten to 150 sheep, from one to ten cows and other domestic animals. Each member is remunerated in accordance with the amount and efficiency of his work. No member of a collective farm can be evicted from it except for crime or flagrant violation of the farm rules and by the vote of at least two-thirds of the collective farm membership. The management of the farm was initially appointed by the government; now it is democratically elected by the farm community for a specific term. The land of the farm cannot be taken from the community, sold, or become an object of profiteering on the part of commercial dealers. As compared with the status of an American tenant, sharecropper, agricultural laborer, or even farm-owner with his farm mortgaged and in danger of fore-closure, the property rights of the Russian peasants are greater and their position is more secure than those of the corresponding strata of the American agricultural population.

The corporation economy does not formally exist in Soviet Russia. In fact, however, the American corporate economy is a twin brother of the corresponding subdivisions of the nation-alized industry in Russia. The total nationalized industry in Russia is divided, as in the United States, into big divisions of steel-oil-construction and other industries, each division being managed by its board of governmental directors, similar to the board of directors of a big American corporation. Neither of these boards, as was mentioned before, owns the corporation and its property. The only difference between these boards is that in Russia the directors are appointed by the government and are responsible to the government and the nation while in the United States directors and big executives are pre-sumably appointed or elected by the thousands of owners, that is, the stockholders of the corporations, and are responsible to them. Factually they are placed in their position by the small, often self-perpetuating, oligarchic group of the bigger shareholders and executives. A previous study of American cor-porations by G. Means and A. Berle (*The Modern Corporation and Private Property*, New York, 1932) and the recent study by several experts (E. S. Mason, ed., *The Corporation in Modern Society*, Cambridge, 1960) show that in none of the big Ameri-can corporations do the directors own even five per cent of its property and that this largest sector of the American economy and, indirectly, of the economy of free enterprise is practically managed and controlled—quite independently from its stock-holders—by some one thousand big executives. These features of the American corporation economy make it indeed very simi-lar to the Russian "nationalized economy of corporations," which is ruled and managed by about the same one thousand big executives of the government. Furthermore, the board of directors in this sector of the economy determines the prices of their products and the wages of their employees. In classical capitalism the prices were determined by "the law of supply and demand" in a free competitive market. This characteristic has largely disappeared from the economy of both countries. The American economy based upon corporations has now entered the phase of "administered prices" arbitrarily determined by the agreement of the big executives of the big corporations. And as time goes on, the secondary differences of this sector of the economy tend to become less and less significant from the standpoint of the economic interests of the populations in both countries. (They remain important, of course, for the personal interests of the big executives of both nations.) Here again, these sectors of the economy in both countries have grown more and more alike.

Finally, in both countries the government is in business and because of the factors governing expansion and contraction of governmental management of business (explained above) the governmentally managed economy is at the present time practically the largest part of the economy in both countries. During the years of World War II practically the entire economy of each country was managed—directly and indirectly—by its government. In these years, there was hardly any basic difference between the economies of "Communist" Russia and the "capitalist" United States. At the present time, this sector of the economy—legally and factually—is still notably larger in Russia in comparison to the United States. However, in Russia it has tended to be less severe, less rigid, and less centralized than it was at the beginning of the Revolution. In the United States since 1914-20, on the contrary, it has tended to expand even in the time of peace (not counting the extraordinary expansions in the time of World Wars I and II). At the present time direct and indirect regimentation and control by the government production, distribution, and consumption of economic goods, of prices and wages, of export and import, of business prosperity and recession, of labor-management relationships, in brief, of the total economy of the United States, has increased many times in comparison with the situation some thirty or forty years ago. This increase is reflected in a manifold increase in the federal and state budgets, in governmental employees, in armed forces and armaments, in the statutes enacted for regulation of economic relationships, in government-owned factories, laboratories, houses, engineering works, in land, warehouses, nationalized natural resources (like uranium), in agricultural and industrial products and in all sorts of other economic goods. As a matter of fact, the role of the governmentally managed economy of the United States is at the present time about as important as, possibly even more important than the role of the corporation economy in the total economy of this country. Only euphemistically or hypocritically can the economy of the United States be called an economy of free enterprise and, as such, be contrasted to the governmentally managed economy of Soviet Russia or to the largely nationalized economies of England and of some European countries. In all three areas the total economies of Russia and the United States have been rapidly converging to the "mixed" type of economy and have become more and more similar to one another.

This increasing similarity manifests itself in many other forms. Though the total national product of American industry still remains greater and the economic standard of living of the United States population much higher than those of Russia, the differences tend, nevertheless, to be progressively smaller. The contentions of N. S. Khrushchev that during the next seven or so years Russia will surpass the United States in its national production and in its standard of living are boastful and improbable; nevertheless these contentions may turn out to be correct in a more remote future.

Technologically both countries have already become essentially similar to each other. Both nations use similar techniques of production, up to the introduction of the techniques of auto-mation and mass production.

In summary, the mutual converging of both countries to similar "mixed" systems of economy has been rapidly progressing.

K. *Social Relationships*

All the enormously diverse forms of human relationships can be classified into three main categories: (*a*) *familistic*, permeated by mutual love, devotion, and sacrifice, most frequently found in the relationships of the members of a good and harmonious family; (*b*) *free contractual* relationships agreed upon by the parties involved for their mutual advantage and profit, devoid of love, hate, or coercion; (*c*) *compulsory* relationships imposed by one party upon the other against his wishes and interests. Of these three relationships, the familistic is the noblest (morally and socially), the compulsory is the worst, while the contractual occupies the intermediary position.

The proportion of each of these three types in the total net-work of interhuman relationships of a social group varies greatly from society to society, from period to period. If the total net-works of social relationships in the United States and Russia are compared from this standpoint, they show the following differences: The proportion of compulsory relationships in the total network of Russia is still notably greater than in the United States; the number of contractual relationships in the United States is much larger than in Russia; and the proportion of familistic relationship in Russia is tangibly larger than in the United States. In all the Soviet policies of nationalization, collectivization, and partial equalization the moving force has been not only the power of crude coercion and often inhuman regimentation by the government, but also the noble power of familistic motives, wishes, and values, especially of the masses of the Russian population. The establishment and development of familistic relationships in the network of the social relationships of Russia has given the "real hidden power" to Soviet policies of nationalization and collectivization and to the Soviet regime itself. Without this hidden power the Soviet government and its coercive policies would have crumbled long ago.

In the course of some forty-five years since the Russian Revolution the marked differences between the American and Russian networks of social relationships have tended to decrease. On the one hand, the coercive policies of the Soviet government have grown milder and have covered progressively fewer areas of human relationships; familistic and, to a smaller degree, contractual relationships have been increasing at the cost of compulsory ones. On the other hand, in the United States the proportion of familistic relationships has also been growing at the cost of contractual ones. This growth has manifested itself in hundreds of different forms and policies of the so-called welfare state, in the enactment of social security, unemployment insurance, wage-minimums, progressive taxation, old-age insurance, various farm relief measures, in the development of schools and public education, medical care and public health improvements, public housing, highway construction, rural electrification, and other public works, in civil rights legislation, and in a multitude of other measures aimed at amelioration of the vital, mental, moral, and social well-being of the total American population, regardless of the commercial profit of a few individuals or groups. In all these forms familistic relationships have successfully grown for the last few decades in the presumably "capitalist" United States.

The growth of familistic and partly contractual relationships in Soviet Russia at the cost of the compulsory ones and growth of familistic relationships in the United States, mainly at the cost of the contractual ones, mean that in this basic field both countries are moving toward a similar type of interpersonal and intergroup relationships of a predominantly familistic character in various degrees of purity and extension.

L. *Political System*

During the first years of the Communist Revolution there certainly was a great conflict between the political regimes of Russia and the United States. In Russia we had the unlimited, tyrannical, totalitarian dictatorship of the top leaders of the Communist party—a most autocratic government that imposed the most coercive regimentation upon every citizen's mind and body, behavior and relationships, and upon the whole social and cultural life of the nation. The government arbitrarily prescribed what each of its subjects was to eat, drink, and wear; in what place and room he had to live; what kind of work he had to do; what he had to read or listen to; what he had to say and believe, approve and disapprove; whether he might be free or imprisoned, whether he might live or be executed. In brief, the government attempted to turn its subjects into mere puppets completely controlled by dictators. This super-totalitarian policy was enforced by the bloodiest and most inhuman coercion—by mass executions of millions of "counter-revolutionaries," by imprisonment of many more millions of stubborn opponents, in jails and concentration camps, by confiscation of their property, and by infliction of all sorts of punishment upon all those who did not comply with the orders of the government. In the whole of human history there have not been many cases of so tyrannical, so super-totalitarian, and so inhumanly autocratic a government. Such a regime naturally conflicted with the democratic order of the United States, with its elective government, its Constitution and Bill of Rights, with the freedom and inalienable rights of every citizen. The basic values of the two political systems were indeed irreconcilable.

However, in the course of subsequent years, a series of important changes has taken place, especially in the Soviet political system. The main trend of these changes has consisted, in Russia, in a progressive limitation of the despotism and super-totalitarianism of the Soviet government and in the expansion of freedom for the Soviet citizens. In the United States it has consisted, rather, in an opposite process right up to the present time, namely, in the expansion of governmental regimentation, censorship, and control of the political ideologies and behavior of its citizens, in the respective decrease of their freedoms and inalienable rights, and in an increase of totalitarian tendencies in its internal and international policies. This totalitarian trend has been due mainly to the transformation from the previous, merely national government into the most powerful empire on the earth. No country or government can escape some degree of totalitarianization when it grows, especially in a short period of time, from the status of one of the important states and governments into that of the most powerful empire or government. Such a transformation is usually accompanied by an increase of various exigencies, particularly the struggle for the maintenance of the position as the greatest world power which inevitably entangles such a country in an endless series of diplomatic and military conflicts with other governments and particularly, in this case, with the Soviet government. This in turn generates a number of other political, economic, social, and moral emergencies for such a country and government, which reinforce the increase of governmental regimentation and control.

Such, in brief, are the main trends in the political systems of both countries. In Russia, the indicated "liberative trend" manifested itself in a multitude of legal and factual changes. Legally, the Constitution of Soviet Russia is one of the most democratic constitutions of the world: among other things, it guarantees all the important freedoms and inalienable rights of man and citizen. The arbitrary despotism of the government, particularly of the secret police, has now been largely replaced by the rule of law with its due process. Executions, imprisonments, and other severe punishments of the opponents of the Soviet government have greatly decreased. Seventy per cent of the concentration camps with slave labor have been dismantled and in the remaining camps the regime is now more humane, offering better food, housing, and working conditions. By a series of laws (April 14, 1957, and others) the citizens are better protected from arbitrary measures of government agents. A large part of the political offenders have been amnestied.

Political offenders are now only about two per cent of the total prison population of Russia. Though the provisions of the Constitution guaranteeing the freedoms and rights of the citizens are still violated occasionally by the government, nevertheless the citizens enjoy much greater freedom and independence than they did at the beginning of the Revolution. Formally, according to the Constitution, the Soviet government is a democratic government, elected by the population. But, due to a one-party system and only one set of candidates nominated by the Communist party, to be voted for or against by the population, the elective character of the government still remains largely nominal. To a great extent, the Soviet government is still the government appointed by the Communist party and its leaders. Nevertheless, in many ways—tangible and intangible—the population exerts a much stronger influence than before upon the elections and upon the government itself. With the passing of the Revolution from its destructive phase, the government progressively has replaced its destructive policies with constructive ones. In its gigantic reconstruction, it has shown a great deal of capable and farsighted leadership devoted to the real interests of the population and to the national interests of Russia. As a result of these policies, it has gained increasing support from the peoples of Russia. At the present time its power is based not so much upon fear and terror—as it was in the destructive phase of the Revolution—as upon the free support and approval of a majority of Soviet citizens. If, hypothetically, the government and its policies were submitted to a really free vote of the population, they probably would receive an endorsement from a majority of the voters. In this sense it can style itself a democratic government or the government of "a people's democracy."

These sketches show clearly the main trend in the change of

the political system of Russia. It can be summed up as moving from an unlimited totalitarian despotism to an increasingly democratic and constructively responsible government which is the leader and servant of the Russian population.

Since its beginning the political system and government of the United States have represented one of the best democratic regimes known to the history of mankind. During the last forty years, they have progressed in many ways toward a still better and "familistic" democracy serving the nation and the world at large. These positive achievements and tendencies have been unfortunately marred by several totalitarian tendencies, due to the indicated factors of the elevation of the United States to the position of the most powerful empire and to a series of wars and other important emergencies hardly avoidable in the process of such a rapid elevation. These totalitarian tendencies manifested themselves not only in the enormous expansion of government control and the regimentation of economic and other spheres of sociocultural life, discussed above, but also in many national and international government policies and in various changes in the political system of the nation. Having declared a "holy crusade" against communism and its alleged "world domination," which practically meant a belligerent crusade against the Soviet government, the Russian nation, and against all other Communist regimes, the American government has involved itself and the American nation in the inevitable consequences of such a policy. By compulsory draft, it had to expand the American armed forces far beyond peacetime proportions. And this expansion of army, navy, and air force to almost three million drafted men means an enormous step in the totalitarianization of the country, since the organization of the armed forces is the most totalitarian of all social groups. The whole life and behavior of a soldier is completely controlled and to the smallest detail regimented by the military code and by his superiors. The commander in chief or any superior officer in battle can send thousands of soldiers to death. The food, drink, uniform, living quarters and all the activities during every twenty-four hour period are rigidly prescribed for members of the armed forces. Their bodies and souls do not belong to themselves but to the armed forces, their superiors, and the nation. For this reason, notable expansion of these forces in any country means a notable expansion of military totalitarianism in the total political system of the country. It is but natural that with this expansion the influence of the supreme military authorities upon the whole political life and the policies of the nation also increases. These inevitably become stamped with the features of "a military (or Pentagon) totalitarianism"—a twin brother to all, including the Communist, totalitarianisms.

The cold and hot wars with the Communist bloc of nations led to legal and factual outlawing of all Communist organizations, to open prosecution of all Communists and "fellow-travelers," and to "hidden" discrimination, disfranchisements, and actual punishment not only of the Communist but of many non-Communist organizations acting as "fronts," and of a multitude of non-Communists, sometimes even anti-Communists, as "fellow-travelers," "sympathizers," "subversives," and "traitors." In these and other ways, a number of American citizens have been intimidated and limited in their freedoms and inalienable rights. These policies of the American government have been but a reversed replica of the totalitarian policies of the Soviet government in regard to the anti-Communists and "subversive" non-Communists. On a still larger scale, the totalitarian tendencies have manifested themselves in the increased official and semi-official demands for "the conformity" of citizens to prescribed patterns of political thought and political behavior; in fostering "guilt by association"; in denunciation and persecution under the pretext of "contempt of Congress" or of a court for all those who have "deviated" from the officially approved modes of conformity; in imprisonment and internment in concentration camps for many "conscientious objectors" and religious nonconformists; in an expansion of the inquisitorial functions of various congressional committees, such as the Committee on un-American Activities, the Committee on National Security, and others which in their procedures and policies often remind one of the worst inquisitorial agencies of the early Soviet regime. By the zealous pursuit of their security tasks these American agencies have even degraded and given a derogatory meaning to the First and the Fifth Amendments to the Constitution of the United States, disdainfully calling "Fifth Amendment subversives" all those who in their own defense have referred to these amendments for protection of their freedom of speech or press.

Fortunately, the development of these totalitarian tendencies has met strong resistance on the part of the American public and, so far, has been moderate and limited. Despite the increase of these tendencies in the United States and their decrease in Soviet Russia, the political system of the United States still remains freer and much more democratic than the Soviet system. However, the difference between these regimes is progressively narrowing and both systems are converging to some intermediary type combining the features of democracy and totalitarianism, familism and Caesarism, freedom and autocratic leadership.

Due to these increasing similarities, the two nations have become more and more alike in the election of their governments and in their party systems. As mentioned before, both governments are elective; but in Russia, with its one-party system, the citizens can only vote "for or against" the candidates nominated by only one—the Communist—party. In the United States we have a two-party system and can vote for the candidates of either the Democratic or the Republican party (the candidates of other minor parties have no chance to be elected to the top positions of federal and state governments). However, the difference between the Democratic and the Republican parties has now become so small and intangible that as a rule it is less significant than the difference between "the left wing" and "the right wing" members of the same party. This means that in fact this country has been evolving toward a one-party system functioning under two different names. For this reason in these basic features of political regime both countries have tended to become more and more similar.

The same is to be said of their international policies. In their unnecessary and unfortunate cold war, with its armament race, its useless waste of the natural resources, of human energy and life (in one Korean "police action" the total number of the victims was larger than in all the Napoleonic wars), with the pending danger of the nuclear, chemical, and bacteriological warfare, both countries are pursuing almost identical policies of using all available means to damage and destroy the other country and its government. All divine and human laws, all moral principles, and the provisions of international law limiting warfare are practically disregarded by both governments. Both governments repeatedly declare that they are ready and willing to kill hundreds of millions of noncombatant civilians, to turn into an "abomination of desolation" cities and villages, to poison all the sources of food and drink, and if need be, to make this planet uninhabitable for the human race as well as for other forms of life. Both governments in their propaganda liberally preach similar high-sounding sermons on justice, peace, freedom, democracy, truth; and now and then they even quote the Sermon on the Mount or other great gospels of the most sublime love and unselfish mutual aid. Both governments likewise try to recruit by all available decent and indecent means all sorts of allies for this suicidal enterprise. In this recruiting business both governments magically transform all the feudal, autocratic, and oligarchic political regimes of the recruited governments into "free" and "democratic" governments, or into the regimes of "a people's democracy." As a result of this magic, the dictatorial regimes of Iran, Turkey, Saudi Arabia, Jordan, Formosa, and of all dictatorial regimes of Latin America, of South Vietnam and other countries allied with the United States, in a twinkling of an eye, have become "free and democratic governments" devoted to "freedom and peace with justice," while all the totalitarian and autocratic regimes allied with the Soviet government miraculously have become "people's democracies" and "freedom-loving governments." It is difficult to decide which of the two governments is more cynical and hypocritical in its struggle for power and domination. The real tragedy of this struggle is that it is carried on at the cost of the vital mental, moral, and social well-being of the populations of the two countries and of all mankind; at the cost of all the great universal, and perennial values continuously undermined, degraded, abused and misused in this struggle by the ruling elites of both nations; and, finally, at the cost of the survival of the human race on this planet.

In summary, both the United States and Russia in the political field have been becoming increasingly similar to each other in good as well as in bad characteristics.

5. CONCLUSION   The preceding brief analysis of the changes and tendencies in the main segments of culture, social institutions, systems of values, and the sociocultural life of both nations demonstrates indeed that in all these basic fields both have been becoming increasingly similar to each other and converging mutually toward a mixed type, neither communistic nor capitalistic, neither totalitarian nor democratic, neither materialistic nor idealistic, neither totally religious nor atheistic-agnostic, neither purely individualistic nor collectivistic, neither too criminal nor too saintly. At the present time this mixed type represents an eclectic mixture of the characteristics of both countries devoid of the unity of the new integral cultural, social, and personal system.

If a peaceful and unimpeded government of today's mixed type is given a real chance, there is hardly any doubt that eventually it will grow into a unified type of a magnificent integral order in both countries as well as in the whole universe. Each country will build this new order in its own variation and each variation is likely to be nobler, more creative, and better than most of the previous sociocultural orders in human history. Viewed in this light, this convergence is a hopeful symptom and a healthy process. As such it can be heartily welcomed by all who really care about man, culture, and all the immortal values created by man on this planet.

The survey also shows that at the present time, among all the different values of the two nations, there is not a single value which justifies the continuation of the present belligerent policies, and absolutely no value which in the smallest degree can redeem the great crime of starting a new world war. This does not mean that such a war cannot be started: Despite his great progress, man still remains, to a considerable extent, an irrational, passionate, destructive, cruel, and greedy creature; and human wickedness still remains rampant in human beings and especially in the ruling groups. If the present destructive struggle between the two countries and the two blocs of nations is continued, and if, especially, a new world war is started, the real reasons for these catastrophes are to be found not in the high-sounding great values invoked by the culprits of the world conflagration, but in our own stupidity, irrationality, greed, irresponsibility, and plain human wickedness.

CHAPTER FOUR

Religious and Moral Polarization of Our Time

1. UNIFORMITY OF THE POLARIZATION IN CRISES   The West and mankind in general are now in a most critical situation threatening the very existence of the human race. This catastrophic feature of our time decisively determines the central characteristic of the present religious and moral situation. A careful investigation of the influence of great national, social, and political catastrophes upon the religious and moral life of individuals and societies shows that, contrary to the two prevalent theories, this influence consists neither in a revival of religiosity and moral ennoblement nor in a mere increase of irreligiosity and demoralization, but rather in the ethico-religious polarization of respective populations. In this polarization, both of these opposite movements coexist and grow at the cost of the customary, routine, somewhat shallow, religiosity and morality of the majority of populations during normal times. This majority, under normal—especially prosperous—conditions, is neither too sinful and irreligious nor too saintly and religious. In the times of great crises, exemplified by wars, revolutions, famines, pestilences, earthquakes, floods, and other catastrophes, this majority tends to polarize: A part of it becomes more religious and moral while another part tends to be more irreligious and criminal. In this way the majority decreases in favor of both opposite poles of intensified religiosity versus militant atheism

and heroic morality versus demoralization. Elsewhere* I have given sufficient historical, empirical, and logical evidence to corroborate this uniformity. The polarization has regularly occurred in practically all the great crises, calamities, and catastrophes in the life-history of past and in recent societies as well as in the lives of ordinary individuals and historical personages.

Usually the negative polarization prevails over the positive in the first period of calamitous times, while the positive polarization becomes prevalent in the latter part of the critical period and after its termination, provided that the society involved does not perish from catastrophic conditions.

From 1914 to this time man has been, and still is, in possibly the most critical period of his entire history. Just now, under a very real threat of suicidal incineration, man's ethico-religious polarization has become gigantic. It manifests itself in all spheres of his social, cultural, and personal life. Particularly tremendous and still prevalent is the negative, ethico-religious polarization.

2. NEGATIVE RELIGIOUS POLARIZATION   From thousands of manifestations of an extraordinary growth of irreligiosity and decline especially in institutional forms of religion, the following essential symptoms can be mentioned:

(a) An enormous growth and diffusion of various forms of atheism among tens of millions of the populations of Communist countries. There has hardly been so great and so rapid a growth

* See P. Sorokin, *Man and Society in Calamity* (New York: E. P. Dutton & Co., 1942), chs. 10, 11, 12. P. Sorokin, *The Ways and Power of Love* (Boston: Beacon Press, 1954), Ch. 12. Our investigation shows that different individuals, beginning with criminals condemned to death and ending with historical persons, react differently to catastrophic and adverse conditions. Some become less religious and moral, less creative, apathetic, mentally disturbed and suicidal while others become more religious, moral, and creative. Accordingly, the theories which claim either a uniform religious and moral ennoblement of all individuals by adversity or their complete religious and moral degradation, are both untenable; they inflate a partial case into a general uniformity.

of militant and radical atheism in the whole of human history.*

(*b*) A steady growth of various materialistic, agnostic, and related philosophies paralleled by the decline of diverse religious and idealistic *Weltanschauungen* after the thirteenth century. During the medieval centuries in the West, from 500 to 1300 A.D., there was hardly any materialistic system of philosophy; since the thirteenth century both forms of materialism—the hylozoistic and the mechanistic—have steadily grown in the nineteenth and in the twentieth centuries to 12.7 and 23.3 per cent, respectively, of all systems treated in the fullest histories of philosophy. In contrast, the idealistic, philosophical *Weltanschauungen* that formerly dominated completely the medieval West, have declined to 55.9 per cent in the nineteenth and to 40.3 per cent in the twentieth century. If to the materialistic philosophies are added various agnostic, "critical," "positivistic," "naturalistic," and "scientific" philosophies which reject almost all the dogmas of the institutional religions, and which, at best, retire God as Emeritus from the actual control of nature and humanity, then an increase of irreligiosity in this century would appear to be still greater than is shown by a springing up of strictly materialistic philosophies.**

(*c*) This conclusion is reinforced by practically all the studies of actual belief or disbelief in the main religious dogmas and rituals by different parts of the Western population. Already the investigations of Professor J. Leuba (*The Belief in God and Immortality*, Boston, 1916, and his later studies), had disclosed that from forty to sixty per cent of American professors and

---

* Of some 220 million of the Russian population, only some fifty-six million now belong to all Christian and non-Christian historical religions. The overwhelming majority has no affiliation with any institutional religion and must be regarded as religiously indifferent and in considerable part agnostic and atheistic.

** See the detailed data and the methods of computation of these figures in P. Sorokin, *Social and Cultural Dynamics* (New York: 1962), Vol. II, Ch. 4.

. There is a short summary of these data in P. Sorokin, *Society, Culture and Personality* (New York: Cooper Square Publishers, 1962), Ch. 41.

students did not believe in the immortality of soul, the divine nature of Christ, the immaculate conception of Jesus, and in several other dogmas of the Christian religion. Subsequent studies essentially confirmed these results. The recent extensive poll of the populations of various European countries, carried on by the International Research Associates, Inc., discovered that in Italy only fifty-one per cent believe in these dogmas, in Norway only forty-two per cent, in Belgium only thirty-three per cent and in France only thirty per cent; and in Europe as a whole about seventy per cent of its polled samples declared themselves agnostics and disbelievers in these dogmas. All these studies have confirmed an essential decline of belief in the main Christian dogmas and efficacy of religious rituals in the Western population during the twentieth century and particularly during the last few decades.

(*d*) Further evidence of the decline of institutional religiosity is given by the notable and systematic decrease of religious masterpieces in all fields of the fine arts, including architecture, and in the notably weakened role of institutional religion in all of Western social and cultural life. In the field of historically known Western paintings and sculpture (my sample consists of more than one hundred thousand paintings and pieces of sculpture), from the tenth to the fifteenth centuries, religious paintings and sculpture composed from eighty-one to ninety-seven per cent of all the important paintings and sculpture known to the history of these fine arts; then during the subsequent centuries these percentages systematically decreased to sixty-four per cent in the sixteenth, and to fifty, twenty-four, ten, and four per cents, respectively in the seventeenth, eighteenth, nineteenth and twentieth centuries.* Similarly, in the field of great Western music, great medieval music was almost one hundred per cent religious; after the twelfth century its percentage began to decrease systematically to forty-two per cent in the seventeenth

---

* See the detailed tables and sources in P. Sorokin, *Social and Cultural Dynamics,* Vol. 1, chs. 5-13.

and eighteenth centuries, to twenty-one per cent in the nineteenth, and to five per cent in the twentieth century. Similarly,
in architecture almost all the great buildings of the Middle
Ages were cathedrals, churches, monasteries, and abbeys. These
buildings dominated the skylines of villages and cities. During
the last few centuries the domination of religious buildings has
been systematically replaced by that of secular buildings—palaces
of secular rulers, mansions of the rich and powerful, town halls,
business buildings, theaters, railroad stations, etc. Amid such
structures as the Empire State Building, the Chrysler Building,
Radio City Music Hall, and the towers of the great metropolitan
dailies, even the vast cathedrals of our cities are lost. A similar
trend has taken place in literature, drama, theater, movies, and
television. The great medieval literature and plays were almost
one hundred per cent religious. Their heroes were divine and
spiritual beings—God, angels, saints. This literature dealt with
the transcendant mysteries of creation, incarnation, redemption,
resurrection, the salvation of human souls, and similar subjects.
After the twelfth century the proportion of grand religious literature tended to decrease progressively until in the present
century it has become an insignificant fraction of today's literature, plays, and theater, not to mention movies, television, and
radio entertainment. Parallel with this secularization, the realm
and personages of literature have descended from the Kingdom
of God to that of the semi-divine hero exemplified by the Ar-
thurian Knights of the Round Table, then to that of ordinary
human beings, and finally, in the twentieth century, into the
subsocial sewers of the criminal, the insane, and the pathological.

A similar decline has taken place in the field of Western ethics
and law. The ethics of absolute moral principles and of unselfish
Christian love and the sacred law systematically declined from
one hundred per cent in the period of 400 to 1400 A.D. to a mere
fifty-seven per cent in the twentieth century, while the secular,
utilitarian, hedonistic, relativistic ethics, absent in the period of
400-1400 A.D., has grown to some forty-three per cent of all ethical

systems in the twentieth century. Sacred law, based upon the commandments of God, has practically disappeared in the twentieth century, to be replaced by purely secular law codes.

Finally, institutional religions in their practical influence and prestige have largely been replaced by science, and by its effective control of the social life, mind, and behavior of individuals and groups.

The separation of Church and State and the declaration of religion as a private affair; the replacement of Church by State in sanctioning births, marriages, and deaths; the elimination of religious education from public schools, up to the recent decision of the Supreme Court of the United States declaring even prayers in school unconstitutional—these and a legion of similar facts additionally confirm the decline of institutional religiosity in recent times.

The totality of the mentioned trends, together with many which remain unmentioned, make the trend of a declining institutional religiosity or of a rising irreligiosity in the twentieth century fairly certain. Whether we want it or not, the negative religious polarization of our time is unquestionable. It has taken place not only in the "atheistic" Communist countries but to a hardly lesser extent in the so-called Christian countries of the West.

3. NEGATIVE MORAL POLARIZATION   In periods of great crisis negative religious polarization is ordinarily associated with negative moral polarization. Since a set of moral commandments is an integral and most important part of any religion—in some of the "humanistic" religions it is their central value—it is natural that the contemporary decline of religiosity has been followed by an enormous upsurge of demoralization in the West. An examination of the Western morality of the twentieth century, from 1914 to the present time, quite definitely confirms this expectation. The actual behavioral morality of the West has sunk during this period to one of the lowest levels in the

whole of human history. Of a multitude of evidential facts of the demoralization I shall mention only a few important categories. They alone are sufficient to prove the point.

(*a*) As mentioned before, the main moral and legal norms of conduct in the Middle Ages were regarded as God-given, absolute norms unconditionally binding upon everyone and everything. After the fifteenth century they began to be increasingly considered as mere human conventions, relative and changeable according to the circumstances and justifiable only from purely utilitarian or hedonistic standpoints. In the twentieth century this relativization of all moral values resulted in their utter atomization and in the loss of their sanctity, their own prestige, and value.

> More and more present-day ethical values are looked upon as mere "rationalizations," "derivations," or "beautiful speech-reactions" veiling the egotistic interests, pecuniary motives, and acquisitive propensities of individuals and groups. Legal norms, likewise, are increasingly considered as a device of the groups in power for exploiting other, more stupid and less powerful groups, a form of trickery employed by the dominant class for subjugation and exploitation of the subordinate classes. Ethical and juridical norms have both become mere rouge and powder to deck out a fairly unattractive body of Marxian economic interests, Paretian "residues," Freudian "libido," the psychologists' "complexes," "drives," and "prepotent reflexes." With the loss of moral prestige, they have progressively forfeited their controlling and binding power. . . . Having lost their "savor" and efficacy, they opened the way for rude force as the only controlling power in human relationships. If neither religious nor ethical nor juridical values control our behavior from within, what then remains? Nothing but naked force and fraud. Hence the contemporary "Might is right." This is the central feature of the crisis in our ethics and law.*

* P. Sorokin, *Society, Culture and Personality* (New York: 1962), p. 628. For details, see also the *Dynamics,* Vol. II, chs. 13, 14, 15.

The actual result of this radical devaluation of the moral and legal values, of their extreme relativization and atomization, has been a general moral confusion, moral anarchy, and the triumph of the principle "Might is right" which is practiced by the leaders as well as by the followers in today's world. This utter demoralization has manifested itself in an unprecedented explosion of international and civil wars, in riots, revolutions, and bloody group conflicts, as well as in the striking demoralization in private, interindividual relationships of the populations of this century. These facts, briefly described, make the gigantic negative moral polarization of our age quite certain.

(b) If the main moral commandment of all religious and ethical systems has been "Thou shalt not kill," then the twentieth century has become the most murderous and most inhuman century of all preceding twenty-five centuries of Greco-Roman and Western history.

In two world wars and in the smaller wars of this century a much greater number of human beings has been killed and wounded than in all the wars of the preceding ten centuries together—a "much greater number" not only in the sense of absolute figures but also in a relative sense of the number of war casualties per one million of the population.*

The same is true of the number of victims of civil wars, revolutions, and important internal disturbances. The twentieth century has turned out to be not only the bloodiest in the international wars but also the most turbulent and most murderous in civil wars and internal conflicts of all the preceding twenty-five centuries of Greco-Roman and Western history. The total number of victims of the Russian and Hitler revolutions ex-

---

* See the detailed statistics of war casualties in all the wars of Greco-Roman and the Western countries from 600 B.C. to present time in P. Sorokin, the *Dynamics*, Vol. III, chs. 9, 10, 11; Q. Wright *A Study of War* (Chicago: Chicago University Press, 1942), 2 vols.; B. L. Urlanis, *Voyny i Narodonaselenie Evropy*, Moscow, 1960. Although differing in details, all these (so far the most substantial) works agree in this conclusion.

ceeds the total number of all revolutions for several preceding centuries of Western history.*

(c) The utter demoralization of the West in the twentieth century has manifested itself not only in the unrivaled murder-ousness of its wars and revolutions, but also in the open and deliberate violation of the restrictions of the divine and human law that prohibits extermination of the noncombatant popula-tion, especially women, children, and old people—a restriction largely obeyed in the wars and revolutions of preceding cen-turies. Two world wars and recent revolutions introduced so-called "total war" in which the total populations of cities, vil-lages, regions, or of "inimical classes" were exterminated, includ-ing noncombatant women, children, and other civilians. In the preceding Victorian age hardly a statesman would have dared to propose such a "total war." After 1914, statesmen, politicians, military and revolutionary leaders began to boast openly of their successful exterminations of the total populations of enemy countries or of social classes. Wars and revolutions have turned into an indiscriminate, wholesale slaughtering of the combatants and noncombatants of an enemy country or social class. In this way not only the commandments of moral law but the restricting provisions of international law have been thrown to the winds. Despite all pompous declarations of the sacredness of human life and the dignity of individuals, human beings have been exterminated more pitilessly in our time than in any previous time, in totalitarian as well as democratic countries.

(d) No wonder, therefore, that at the present time the gov-ernments and power-elites of the Western and the Soviet blocs of nations are feverishly and openly preparing for incineration through a third world war. They unblushingly declare their eagerness to use all nuclear, chemical, and bacteriological means

* See the detailed statistics of the number of victims of all the civil wars, revolutions, and important internal disturbances in Greco-Roman and the Western history from 600 B.C. to the present time in P. Sorokin, *Dynamics,* Vol. III, chs. 12, 13; and B. L. Urlanis, *op. cit.,* pp. 180ff.

of warfare for indiscriminate extermination of hundreds of millions, possibly even of the whole human race. Insofar as such devilish policies of the governments are supported by a considerable part of their populations, this fact alone signifies that the public morality of these nations has reached its most insanely low level or the extreme limit of demoralization beyond which one cannot go except in actual accomplishment of the wholesale extermination of the human race.

(*e*) If in the wars, revolutions, and other intergroup conflicts of the twentieth century the gravest form of crime—the murder of man by man—has increased to an unprecedented height, the same is true of other lesser crimes against persons, good mores, and property rights. Mass-scale deprivation of freedom in the form of mass-imprisonment, concentration camps, banishment, etc., the infliction on enemies of various—physical and mental—tortures, rape and other sex-offenses, large-scale confiscation of property, and other instances of inhumanity—all these violations of moral and legal provisions have been perpetrated in the wars, revolutions, and other violent intergroup conflicts of this century on an unprecedented scale. They have often been perpetrated with coldblooded, "scientific" bestiality. "The worst of the beasts" in man has been unleashed to a degree hardly rivaled in the past, and Man the Killer and Destroyer has become the "star" of the historical tragedy of our time.

(*f*) This apocalyptic demoralization in intergroups or public relationships has naturally been paralleled by a gigantic demoralization in the interpersonal or private relationships of individuals. Out of hundreds of forms of this private demoralization the following classes can be mentioned here:

(1) A systematic increase of interindividual criminality—juvenile and adult—in almost all Western countries.

(2) An increase of mental disease, drug addiction, suicide, and *anomie* by the victims of moral anarchy.

(3) An increase of moral cynicism, corruption, gross sensualism of the type "Eat, drink, and be merry for tomorrow we die" in governmental and private circles of the populations.

(4) Increasing violations of contractual obligations by private individuals, by governments, by labor and management, and by all sorts of groups and unions. The old binding *pacta sunt servanda* is largely forgotten, and a legion of individuals and groups are unhesitatingly violating their contractual duties as soon as a profitable occasion for such violations arises. Among other violators, all the existing governments, without exception, have proved themselves "chronic double-crossers."

(5) This sort of violation has also deeply penetrated the realm of marriage and family relationships, as evidenced by a great and systematic increase of divorces, separations, and desertions, and by an increase of premarital and extra-marital sex liaisons.

Even omitting a long series of other proof of gigantic demoralization, this succession of ugly facts makes it hardly questionable. We indeed live in an age of tremendous negative moral polarization rarely if ever rivaled in the past history of mankind.

4. Positive Religious Polarization   If the present religious and moral situation were marked only by the outlined negative polarization, a greater part of mankind would have already perished in the intergroup and interindividual *bellum omnium contra omnes;* the nuclear, the chemical, and the bacteriological world wars would have already exploded, and in the pitiful remaining part of the human race no decent order or decent life could have survived and continued to function. If this tragic finale has not occurred as yet, this has been largely due to the resistance by the forces of positive religious and moral polarization to the destructive work of the forces of negative polarization. The destructive action of the latter seems to have been somewhat limited and neutralized by the constructive counteraction of the former.

A factual survey of the religious and moral phenomena of our age shows indeed that, along with the explosion of the forces of negative polarization, there appeared and are growing the forces of a positive religious and moral polarization. Though at the present time the forces of the negative polarization are still prevalent, those of the positive polarization are already quite visible. If the forces of negative polarization do not succeed within a decade or so to produce the universal incineration of mankind, the constructive religious and moral forces are bound to grow, eventually to become prevalent over the destructive forces, and to build a new social, cultural, and personal order in the human universe. Such has been the way out of many great crises in the past (when the societies involved in the crises did not perish and did manage to overcome their critical states) * and such is to be the way out of the present perilous state of mankind. Let us briefly glance at some of the manifestations of the positive polarization of our age.

(a) One of the evidences of the polarization is given by the Russian population. Despite all the severe persecution of religions in the first period of the revolution, despite some disfranchisements that religious affiliation still has there, despite a militant crusade of atheism, there are still some fifty million members of the Russian Orthodox Church; some five million members of the Protestant denominations; several millions of Catholics, Mohammedans, Jews, and members of other institutionalized religions, with their churches; thousands of priests and divinity schools; not to mention millions of religiously minded persons—mystics, gnostics, etc., who are not affiliated with institutional religions. And, as time goes on, the number of such religious persons is growing rather than decreasing. This survival and growth of religiosity under extremely adverse conditions has been possible only through an enormous intensification, purification, and spiritualization of the religiosity of these

* See the historical facts in P. Sorokin, *Man and Society in Calamity*, quoted, chs. 10-13.

millions.* The mere routine, superficial religiosity of normal times would have been incapable of standing the persecutions, disfranchisements, and atheistic attacks upon it and would have succumbed under the gigantic pressure of anti-religious forces, as indeed happened to many millions of the Russian population who are now irreligious or indifferent at least in regard to the institutionalized forms of religion.

Due largely to this positive polarization, the persecution of religions, *qua* religions, has practically ceased at the present time; the autonomy of all the institutionalized religious authorities in religious matters is legally and factually established; even the principal expenses of the Patriarchy of the Russian Orthodox Church are paid by the Soviet State.

Atheistic propaganda has greatly decreased. Even the philosophy of dialectical materialism, as a background for atheistic ideologies, has become notably more idealistic than it was at the beginning of the revolution. Except for materialistic terminology, it is nearer to Hegelian objective idealism and in a number of points to the Platonic or Thomistic philosophies than to "vulgar" mechanistic materialism (as the Soviet philosophers of dialectical materialism call it).**

(*b*) In the United States (and in several other countries) positive religious polarization has manifested itself by an increase in the membership of the institutionalized religions, from forty-seven per cent of the population fourteen years and over in 1926, to sixty-three per cent in 1960; in an increase of financial

---

* During the first years of the revolution I personally witnessed this intensification and spiritualization of the religiosity of the faithful: it was very similar to that of the early Christians ready to suffer for their religious values; the atmosphere of the religious services held in a few remaining churches were reminiscent of the services in the early Christian catacombs.

** See the preceding chapter, *Mutual Convergence of the United States and the U.S.S.R. to the Third Mixed Sociocultural Type.* This essay was also published in German translation in the *Zietschrift fur Politik,* December, 1960, and in Spanish translation in P. Sorokin, *Convergencia de Estados Unidos y la U. R. S. S.,* Costa-Amie, Mexico, 1961.

contributions to religious institutions, in the erection of religious buildings, and other symptoms of religious development.

(c) A still more important symptom of this polarization is the growth of noninstitutionalized religiosity and of an intensified search for the ultimate reality and supreme values. The growth of noninstitutionalized religiosity is shown, among other things, by the emergence and multiplication of various spiritual sects and altruistic moral groups of the "high-brow" (such as "humanist" and "ethical" groups) and of the "low-brow" (Jehovah's Witnesses, etc.) types. These sects and groups take their religion and its moral precepts much more seriously than do routine believers of the established religions in normal times. They regard their religious values as sacred and inviolable, and they try to realize them and their moral commandments not only in verbal preaching but especially in their overt actions.

As to the search for the supreme reality and values which are the central problems of all religions, despite a lack of statistical data of the number of persons engaged in it, it is reasonably certain that this sort of search is going on now in millions of souls of our fellowmen. The general insecurity of our time (particularly that of the pending universal incineration); disillusionment with transient and precarious material values; skepticism and disbelief in the dogmas and rituals of the old religions; the rampant blood conflicts of wars, revolts, and internal disturbances; the tragically sad economic, political, social, and general situations of many groups and millions of individuals; a general spirit of unrest and revaluation of all values—these and many other conditions are forcing millions of individuals to search for new or to try to rediscover the old, supreme values and imperishable realities. Despite its intangibility this search is perhaps the most significant manifestation of positive religious and moral polarization. It is exactly from such a search in the past that all the great religions emerged as new answers to the tragic problems of their times and societies. And it is highly probable that, from the present search for the new or for rediscovery of the old ultimate verities, new prophets and new creators of the future great religions will appear. Herein lies the particular significance of this quest of millions of human souls in our time.

(*d*) Further signs of the positive polarization are: (1) the invigorated evangelical preachings and teachings exemplified by the successful campaigns of many religious leaders; (2) the numerous conversions achieved by their activities; (3) utilization of modern means of communication, such as radio, television, movies, and the press for religious purposes; (4) the notably increased number of religious publications and periodicals; (5) various special efforts of the clergy to discharge their duties more faithfully and competently, including the scientific training necessary for that purpose; (6) a better organization of religious bodies for a more efficient and effective performance of their functions, and several other improvements of the clergy, religious organizations, and their activities.

(*e*) A more important symptom of this polarization appears in the cooperation and unification of various Christian and other denominations in their concerted religious work. In this work they now stress the common values of different religions much more than their differences and "superiorities." This trend notably weakens the largely fruitless interdenominational rivalries and reinforces the task of religious education of mankind in the basic, common values of all religions. Among its positive results it has led to mergers of several denominations, to concerted work and the organization of several interreligious agencies culminating in the World Council of Churches, the Ecumenical Religious Conferences, and the World Congresses of Religions. This unification and cooperation in the spirit of the Vedantic motto: "God is One but men call it by different names," has already yielded many significant results.

These and many other movements make the emergence and growth of positive religious polarization fairly certain. Though it seems to be still notably weaker than is negative polarization, nevertheless, the very fact of a tangible institutional and non-institutional religious revival in our time is fairly visible and real.

5. POSITIVE MORAL POLARIZATION   The same can be said about the positive moral polarization of our time. (*a*) As a counter-reaction to the murderous wars, bloody conflicts, and pending threat of a new world war, thousands of anti-war organizations in all countries have sprung up and are rapidly developing their activities. Beginning with the United Nations and ending with numerous pacifistic and nonviolent groups and associations—local, national, and international—these forces of peace and morality are already exerting quite a powerful influence upon the governments and other agencies of militarism, organized murder, and violence. War and bloody violence as the means of settling intergroup or interindividual conflicts are already largely discredited morally. Hardly any time in the past has there been in the whole body of mankind such an aversion to these violent means and such a diffusion of nonviolent resistance to evil as can be observed at the present time. An ever-increasing part of the human population, with ever-greater determination is endeavoring to eliminate from human history the shame of wars and to realize the greatest moral imperative "Thou shalt not kill," as well as other universal and perennial moral precepts.

If a new apocalyptic world incineration has not exploded up to the present time, it is largely due to the mobilization and activities of these moral forces. Factually and potentially they represent perhaps the most important form of positive moral polarization.

(*b*) Another manifestation of positive polarization is the financial and nonfinancial help which is unselfishly rendered by many governments and public and private agencies to groups and persons in urgent need of such help. The United States alone has spent many billions of dollars for the "backward countries" and for many other groups needing assistance. Large sums are being spent for that purpose by other countries. In addition to financial help, technical, scientific, and cultural assistance is liberally given by many groups and agencies to the nations and groups in a need of it. This kind of altruistic activity has now reached a degree rarely, if ever, rivaled before.

(*c*) The same is true of the unselfish actions rendered by individuals to other individuals. Though such moral deeds are much less publicized than are individual aggressive actions, nevertheless they are performed daily by millions of individuals in regard to each other. Almost any aggressive and bestial inter-individual act of our time is countered by an unselfish act, often involving great sacrifice and now and then reaching the height of moral heroism.

(*d*) Even in the political field, where the policy "might is right" has been particularly practiced and where negative polarization has been especially strong, positive polarization has developed and has already achieved many positive results, such as the liberation of almost all colonial peoples from their colonial servitude, elimination of many racial, ethnic, religious, and other disfranchisements and inequalities, the increase of potential freedom, the mitigation of political corruption and irresponsibility, and other moral consequences.

An ever-increasing portion of mankind is now earnestly endeavoring to build nobler and better forms of political organization and social life, and is succeeding in this task to a considerable extent—and this not only in the Western but no less in the Eastern bloc of nations. Along with the stern regimentation of millions of their citizens, the Soviet and similar regimes have liberated these millions from many forms of subjugation and exploitation which they previously suffered. By their policies of collectivization, nationalization, and partial equalization, these regimes have evoked in their citizens not only the mentality and behavior of regimented and enslaved prisoners, but also the ethos and the conduct of a free, collective "we," spontaneously united into one vast family by sympathy and responsibility, by mutual aid, free cooperation, and unselfish love. In such a community there are few isolated individuals completely engrossed in their selfish pursuits, careless of others, and uncared for by anyone.

In somewhat different form, this task of building a morally and socially nobler order in the human universe is quite vigorously pursued also in the Western bloc of nations. In pursuit of this task both blocs of nations are freeing themselves from the negative and antiquated defects of the so-called capitalist and Communist orders and are moving to a new integral order embodying the real values of both ways of life and organization. Despite the prevalent policies of the governments and politicians of both blocs of nations, still feverishly busy with their "hot and cold wars," this trend has grown progressively. If World War III does not explode in the near future, the trend will certainly continue and will eventually prevail over the destructive, largely antiquated policies of capitalism and communism. The realization of the integral order would mean an epochal moral step forward of mankind in its creative mission on this planet.

(e) Positive polarization has taken place also in the field of scientific theories of moral phenomena. Stimulated by the calamities of this century, a more careful study of these phenomena has led to a drastic revision of many supposedly scientific theories prevalent until recent times and to the replacement of these inadequate "ideologies" by more valid scientific ideas.

(1) First, fashionable ideologies which saw moral phenomena as a mere beautifying screen for economic and other material interests have been found to be inadequate and one-sided. The theories that denied the effectiveness of moral forces in conditioning human behavior, both individual and collective, were also found grossly fallacious.

(2) As a specific detail of these conclusions, the contemporary biological and psychosocial sciences fairly unanimously stress that the moral factors of mutual aid, cooperation, sympathy,

and unselfish love (in its instinctive, rational, and superrational manifestations) have played at least as important a role in the biological and psychosocial evolution of living forms, and especially in the progressive history of the human race, as the hitherto overemphasized factor of the struggle for existence which involves egoistic competition, hate, and brutal force. Recent studies of the role of unselfish, creative love have disclosed that it has been and is a real power which can: (A) stop aggressive interindividual and intergroup attacks; (B) can transform inimical relationships into amicable ones; they have also discovered: (C) that love begets love and hate generates hate; (D) that love can tangibly influence international policy and pacify international conflicts; (E) that love is a life-giving force, necessary for physical, mental, and moral health; (F) that altruistic persons live longer than egoistic ones; (G) that children deprived of love tend to become morally and socially defective; (H) that love is a powerful antidote against criminal, morbid, and suicidal tendencies, against hate, fear, and psychoneuroses; that love performs important cognitive and aesthetic functions; (J) that it is the loftiest and most effective educational force for the enlightenment and moral ennoblement of humanity; (K) that it is the heart and soul of freedom and of all main moral and religious values; (L) that a minimum of love is absolutely necessary for the continuing existence of any society, and especially for a harmonious social order and for creative progress; (M) finally, that at the present catastrophic moment in history an increased "production, accumulation and circulation of love-energy" and a notable altruization of persons, groups, institutions, and culture is a necessary condition for the prevention of new wars and for alleviation of interindividual and intergroup strife.*

---

* See the details and corroborative evidence for these statements in P. Sorokin, *The Ways and Power of Love* (Boston: Beacon Press, 1954). There is also a vast literature about these problems given here. Compare also the subsequent essay, "The Mysterious Energy of Love."

(3) Also all the theories that consider the moral norms and values as mere human conventions that can be changed at will, and all the fashionable ideologies that stress unlimited relativism and atomism are found to be fallacious. A more careful study of moral phenomena (legal codes, mores, folkways, and moral systems) shows that, along with local, temporary, and ever-changing tribal moral and legal norms, there have been certain universal and perennial moral and legal norms that are required to be practiced in *all* societies in regard to their members and which are quite necessary for the maintenance of a good life in any society or individual. The main moral commandments of all great religions, of all legal codes, of all mores and folkways in regard to the respective in-group members, their "Thou shalt" and "Thou shalt nots," are very similar, often identical. Individuals or groups can of course transgress these norms, as they unfortunately do; but for transgressing these moral laws, just as for a violation of the physical laws of nature, they have to pay a heavy price in the form of various disastrous consequences. Because of this, contemporary scientific theories of moral phenomena have largely discredited the pseudo-scientific ideologies of an unlimited moral relativism and atomism and have laid a scientific foundation for the practical construction of a system of universal and perennial moral values that are binding upon everyone and are necessary for the well-being of any group and individual.*

(4) Similar revisions have also recently taken place in regard to the theories of human personality. Man has hitherto been viewed mainly as an animal organism of the Homo sapiens and has been interpreted predominantly in mechanistic, materialistic, reflexological, libidinal, and endocrinological terms. This sort of interpretation contributed to the modern mistreatment of man by man and to the expendability of human life. The new integral theory of human personality does not deny that man

* Compare for development and corroboration of these statements, P. Sorokin, *Dynamics*, quoted, Vol. II, chs. 13, 14 and 15.

is an animal organism endowed with the "unconscious," reflexo-instinctive mechanism of body, but it stresses that besides
this form of being, man is a conscious, rational thinker and a
supraconscious creator or genius (this refers to man's Nous,
Pneuma, Spirit, Soul, or Divine Self). These forms of being
make man an end value in himself and therefore a being who
cannot be treated as a mere means for anything and anybody.*

These and other revisions of scientific theories of moral and
related phenomena are not only one of the manifestations of
positive polarization, but they have laid down scientific, philosophical, and ideological foundations for the construction of a
nobler moral and religious order.

As for the manifestation of positive polarization many other
symptomatic facts can be added. In their totality they demonstrate the reality of this polarization. Though the forces of
negative polarization seem still to be prevailing, nevertheless
those of positive polarization already display a tangible capacity
for inhibiting and mitigating the disastrous operations of the
forces of irreligiosity and demoralization. Together with the
forces of positive religious polarization, they are now engaged
in a momentous struggle with their adversary. This struggle is
one of the very basic conflicts of our time.

6. PROGNOSIS   What is going to be the final result of this
epochal struggle?

Nobody, least of all I, can predict with certainty which of
these forces will be victorious. Mankind of the twentieth century,
especially its power elites, have displayed such Gargantuan folly,
bestiality, and sadistic destructiveness that even an enthusiastic
believer in human progress is tempered in his Candidian opti-
mism. On the other hand, the history of the human race
testifies that it has somehow been able to overcome many
catastrophes during its long historical existence. One thing,

* See on this integral theory of human personality, P. Sorokin, *The
Ways and Power of Love*, chs. 5, 6, and 7.

however, can be said: If the forces of negative polarization decisively prevail, their victory will be marked by the explosion of a new apocalyptic (nuclear, chemical, and bacteriological) world war which will certainly terminate for a long time, if not forever, the mission of man in all the fields of creativity, including the religious and moral ones. In that case a solemn requiem to Homo sapiens would be more appropriate (if anyone remains to sing it) than a learned treatise about the religious and moral consequences of the world incineration.

In cooperation with all the creative agencies, the forces of positive polarization must do their best to prevent this mournful *finis* to human history. In order to accomplish this task and then to be of the important builders of the new cultural, social, and personal order in the human universe, these forces themselves must undergo several important changes and realignments in their strategic activities. Of a large number of such self-transformations and realignments the following ones can be mentioned here:

(*a*) For the present and immediate future all religious and moral forces must exert their utmost influence to prevent the new world war and other bloody conflicts. By doing so they will be fulfilling one of the main commandments of all religious and truly moral systems, namely "Thou shalt not kill." Until now they have often failed in this task; frequently they have even blessed and approved wars, riots, and legitimate murders of various "enemies"; at best they have often preached this precept and rarely practiced it. Even in their preaching they have been anxious to please various "Caesars" rather than God and his moral imperative. Now the time has come when a superficial, semi-hypocritical fulfillment of this imperative will no longer do. By its continuation respective religions and moral systems will either simply make themselves ineffectual or will become one of the many destructive forces of negative polarization. Providence or Destiny has set forth an ultimatum to all religious and moral systems: either they decisively begin to realize this imperative or become the empty shells of previously important creative forces. If, indeed, the religious and moral forces of all denominations would transcend their tribal interests and would wholeheartedly, sometimes even offensively to the powers that be, throw all their weight into the prevention of a new world war and the realization of "Thou shalt not kill," they would fulfill their duty to God and render a tremendous service to humanity. By this service they would demonstrate their own inestimable value and creative capacity. In this way they would become one of the great saviors of mankind and builders of a nobler order.

(*b*) For the same purpose, all religions, old and new, must intensify their work in the field of moral transformation of the overt conduct of their members, of making them not only profess but practice their moral precepts, particularly the main precept "God is Love." Purely verbal and ritualistic religion does not help much to prevent the threatening world incineration, if such an "easy religion" is not implemented by deeds of unselfish love. Jesus, St. James, and St. Paul correctly stated that "faith without works is dead!" Because the systematic practice of the commandment of love—the main commandment of their moral code—is much more difficult than a mere "verbalistic-ritualistic" profession of faith, the truly religious who unfailingly practice their moral commandments have always been an insignificant minority of the members of any religious group. Among millions of Christians there are few who regularly practice most of the precepts of the Sermon on the Mount. The same is true of the followers of other religions with multi-million memberships. The deep chasm between noble preachings and ignoble practices explains the modest results of religions in the prevention and elimination of the bloodiest forms of interhuman strife.

The present, very critical situation of mankind and the deep chasm between noble professions of faith and ignoble practices imperatively demand from all religions the greatest possible concentration on the moral transformation of the human race in the direction of creative and unselfish love, not only preached but practiced. Otherwise, it is doubtful that purely verbalistic and ritualistic religions can become the spiritual and moral leaders in overcoming the gigantic dangers of the present and in building the future order in the human universe. We must not forget that practically all the great religions emerged in catastrophic circumstances and, at their initial period, were first of all and most of all *moral* social movements inspired by sympathy, compassion, and the Gospel of Love. They set out to achieve the moral regeneration of a demoralized society. Only later on did such movements become overgrown by complex theological dogmas and impressive rituals. This is equally true of the emergence of Taoism, Confucianism, Zoroastrianism, Hinduism, Jainism, Buddhism, the Mosaic and the Prophetic Judaisms, Christianity, and other ethico-religious movements. If at their heroic phase these ethico-religious movements greatly helped to overcome the catastrophes in the history of ancient Egypt, Babylonia, China, India, Persia, Israel, Greece, Rome, and of the Western countries, the existing religions together can now perform this task for all of mankind. Since the main moral commandments of all great religions are essentially similar, they can wholeheartedly cooperate in this task of the altruistic transformation of overt behavior, social institutions, and culture of their peoples. It offers them real common ground for such cooperation, allowing each of the religions to maintain the individuality of its own theological dogmas and rituals.

(c) In discharging this task however, the existing religions must replace their hitherto predominant tribal viewpoint with a universal one, in the sense of requiring the practical application of moral precepts not only to the members of one's religion but to all human beings regardless of their religion, race, nationality, social position, sex, age, and other differences. Whether we want it or not, the tribal stage of human history in all its forms is essentially over. The human race has already become, to a large extent, one interdependent whole. Any important change in any important social group—be it a national, state, religious, occupational, racial, or ethnic group, a social class, or any other collectivity—quite tangibly affects the life and well-being of the rest of mankind. The replacement of selfish tribal policies by universal ones is going on even in the constructive policies of states, social classes, and other powerful groups. For religious organizations such a replacement not only is more urgently required but is more easily attainable because the moral commandments of almost all the world religions have been addressed to all human beings, have been universal, not tribal, in their intent. In practice, however, they have often been applied only to the members of a given religion and not to all human beings. With the passing of the tribal stage of human history, the intended universality of their moral imperatives is needed now to be applied in practice. The time of selfishly tribal religions, so far as their moral commandments are concerned, is about over.

(*d*) The replacement of religious tribalism by universalism implies among other things: (1) the abandonment of monopolistic claims of many religions to be the only true religion and to possess indubitable superiority over all other religions, and the abandonment of the policies of religious imperialism with its intolerance, disrespect and persecution of other religions. This last has fairly frequently been practiced in the past by such "imperialistic" religions as Judaism, Christianity, and Mohammedanism (to a lesser degree by the religions of Taoism, Confucianism, Hinduism, Jainism, and Buddhism). In its infinite plenitude the True and Supreme Reality of God still remains the *mysterium tremendum et fascinosum,* the *coincidentia oppositorum,* "the Divine Nothing" into which fade all things and differentiations. In His fullness God can hardly be adequately comprehended by any finite human mind or by any finite human beliefs. For this reason no human religion can claim to have a monopoly on an adequate comprehension of

God, as God's exclusive confidant and agent. On the other hand, the numberless ripples of this Infinite Ocean allow different groups of believers to select those that for various reasons most appeal to them. So understood, the differences in the chosen "ripples," usually reflected in the dogmas and rituals of different religions, in no way necessitate that different denominations be antagonistic to each other or view their own beliefs as the only true ones and those of other religions as totally false. Cherishing their own beliefs, the believers of each religion can equally respect the beliefs of others as supplementary to their own, revealing additional aspects of the *mysterium tremendum et fascinosum*. Viewed so, religious differences cannot only be tolerated but genuinely welcomed and esteemed. In their totality they convey to us a fuller knowledge of the Supreme Reality than that given by a single religion. So considered, they give a solid ground for a wholehearted cooperation of all religions in the great task of "the feeling of the Presence" (in Brother Lawrence's terms), of better knowledge of the "Divine Nothing," and in realization of God's ways in the human world.

Fortunately for us, this sort of cooperation has already started and is rapidly developing. It is represented by such movements and organizations as the World Council of Churches, The Ecumenical Conference called by the Pope, the International Congress of Religions, the Conference of Christians and Jews, the unified activities of Catholics, Protestants, and Jews, by mergers of two or more denominations into one unified religious body, and by similar phenomena. It is very probable that in the near future a truly ecumenical cooperation of all religions, Christian and non-Christian, will grow rapidly and will realize this important task more fully.

(*e*) Along with this cooperation of all religious forces in the spiritual and moral transfiguration of mankind, all religions must also establish a harmonious relationship and wholehearted cooperation with science.

(1) While the verities of their moral codes like the Sermon

on the Mount can hardly be improved by science or need any new discovery, in the techniques of effective inculcation of these precepts into the minds and overt conduct of human beings, religions can be greatly helped by scientific knowledge of the efficacious techniques for transforming human beings and their behavior.*

(2) While in their basic conception of the Supreme Reality (God) religions can be largely independent from science, their theological teachings concerning the empirical manifestations of this reality must reckon with and take into consideration scientific conclusions about empirical phenomena. Science specialized in their study knows more about them than metaphysics, theology, or philosophy. Being truer, science's conclusions concerning the empirical forms of reality cannot be disputed by purely speculative and mythological ideologies still present in dogmas of many religions. This replacement of the obsolescent empirical mythologies in religions by scientific conclusions represents another form of cooperation and harmonization of religions and science.

(3) This cooperation may go further and deeper and may extend even into the field of the basic conceptions of the total and true reality, of the ways of cognition of this reality, and of the true nature of human personality. In these fields science and religion can indeed be mutually helpful. By working together, they can deliver a better knowledge of these basic problems than by working alone or by warring with each other.

---

* As an example of this, the recent cooperation of various religions with psychiatry may be mentioned. However, in this particular case, since many religious agencies have selected Freudian psychiatry and psychology, their choice of this largely pseudo-scientific variety of psychology and therapy is hardly fortunate. Religions themselves have a much more scientific "monastic psychoanalysis," which can be enriched by the knowledge of more sound or scientific types of psychology and psychiatry. See on "monastic psychoanalysis" and various techniques of efficacious transformation of human beings, P. Sorokin, *The Ways and Power of Love,* chs. 16-22; P. Sorokin (ed.), *Forms and Techniques of Altruistic and Spiritual Growth* (Boston: Beacon Press, 1954).

As a matter of fact, the beginnings of such a deeper cooperation have already appeared in our time. This can be seen in the profound changes of today's scientific theories concerning the total reality, the ways of cognition of this reality, and the conception of human personality—changes which have brought today's scientific theories notably nearer to the best religious philosophies concerning these problems.

The same can be said about the recent scientific theories of cognition of reality.* In this integral theory of cognition, the "supersensory-superrational" way is congenial with the "divine revelation" of religions.

Likewise the hitherto dominant, sensate theories of man as an animal organism of the Homo sapiens species whose nature and behavior can be interpreted mainly in mechanistic, materialistic, reflexological, and other "physicalistic" terms, are being rapidly superseded by a more adequate triadic conception of man, which is again congenial to that of many religions.

The above examples illustrate what I mean by a deeper cooperation between science and religion. In this cooperation both become unified into one *Ganzheit* harmoniously working for the greater glory of God and the ennoblement of man.

I have mentioned only a few ways of increasing the growth and creativity of the forces of the positive polarization. If this growth is not interrupted by a new world war and other catastrophes, these forces will certainly prevail over those of the negative polarization; they will eventually usher humanity into a new era of its creative history. In this era it is hoped that spiritually and morally ennobled religion will wholeheartedly cooperate with a morally responsible science and purified and

* Compare for the details of this integral theory of cognition and creativity and for the evidence of functioning of "the supersensory-superrational" method of cognition and creativity, P. Sorokin, *The Ways and Power of Love*, chs. 6, 7, and 8; Sorokin's *Reply* in P. Allen's (ed.) volume *P. A. Sorokin in Review* (Durham N. C.: Duke University Press, 1953), and the preceding essay "Three Basic Trends."

refined arts. Truth, goodness, and beauty will again be united into the highest trinity of values—all unfolding more fully the mysteries of the Supreme Reality and all faithfully serving mankind in its creative mission on this planet and beyond it. Our time is propitious for this magnificent possibility.

CHAPTER FIVE

The Mysterious Energy of Love*

1. THE NEW FIELD OF RESEARCH   In recent decades science has opened several new fields for exploration and use. The probings into the subatomic world and the harnessing of atomic energy are but two examples of these ventures. Perhaps the latest realm to be explored is the mysterious realm of altruistic love. Though now in its infancy, its scientific study is likely to become a most important area for future research.

Before World War I and the later catastrophes of our time science largely shunned this field. The phenomena of altruistic love were thought to belong to religion and ethics rather than to science. They were considered good topics for sermons but not for research and teaching. Moreover, prewar science was much more interested in the study of criminals than of saints, of the insane than of the genius, of the struggle for existence than of mutual aid, and of hate and selfishness than of compassion and love.

The explosion of the gigantic disasters after 1914 and the pending danger of a new suicidal war have now radically changed this situation. These calamities have given impetus to the scientific study of unselfish love. They have also led to basic revisions of many theories until now regarded as scientific, and especially those which dealt with the causes and means of prevention of wars, revolutions, and crime.

* A full development and corroboration of all statements of this essay can be found in P. Sorokin, *The Ways and Power of Love* (Boston: Beacon Press, 1954).

The Mysterious Energy of Love

Among other things these revisions have shown that without reinforcement by the energy of unselfish love, all the fashionable prescriptions for elimination of the ills of humanity cannot achieve their task. This conclusion equally applied to all the prescriptions that try to prevent conflicts by either purely political, educational, sham-religious, economic, or military means. For instance, we may like to think that if tomorrow all the governments in the world were to become democratic, we would finally have a lasting peace and a crimeless social order. Yet recent careful studies of comparative criminality, of 967 wars and 1629 internal disturbances in the history of Greece, Rome, and the Western countries since 600 B.C. up to the present time show that democracies have hardly been less belligerent, turbulent, and crime-infested than autocracies.*

Moreover education in its present form has not been a panacea for international wars, civil strife, and crime. From the tenth century to the present time education has made enormous strides forward. The number of schools of all kinds, the percentage of literacy, and the number of scientific discoveries and inventions have greatly increased. Yet the number and deadliness of wars, bloody revolutions and grave crimes have not decreased. On the contrary, in this most scientific and most educated twentieth century they have reached unrivaled heights and have made this century the bloodiest in the past twenty-five centuries of Greco-Roman and Western history.**

Similarly, the tremendous progress of knowledge and domestication of all forms of physical energy has not given man lasting peace. Rather, it has greatly increased his chances of being destroyed in all forms of interhuman conflict.

Even shallow—purely verbalistic and ritualistic—religion does not help much in this task, if such an "easy" religion is not implemented by deeds of unselfish love. Jesus, St. James, and St.

---

* See the evidence in the *Dynamics*, quoted, Vol. III, chs. 9-14.
** See the evidence in P. Sorokin, *Reconstruction of Humanity* (Boston: Beacon Press, 1948), chs. 1-3.

Paul quite correctly stated that "faith without works is dead" and that "in Jesus neither circumcision availeth anything, nor uncircumcision; but faith which worketh by love." As systematic practice of the commandments of love is much more difficult than a mere "verbalistic-ritualistic" profession of faith, the truly religious, who unfailingly practice their moral commandments, have always made up an insignificant minority of the members of any religious group. Among millions of Christians there are few who regularly practice such precepts of the Sermon on the Mount as: "love your enemies, do good to them that hate you," "whosoever shall smite thee on thy right cheek, turn to him the other also," or most of the other precepts of this Sermon. The same is true of the followers of other religions with multi-million memberships. When we investigated seventy-three converts of a popular evangelist, we found out that only one of these "mass-assembly line converts" had tangibly changed his overt behavior in an altruistic direction. This deep chasm between noble preachings and ignoble practices explains the modest results of religions in the prevention of strife. Since this chasm seems to have deepened during the last few centuries there is little chance for the verbalistic religions to achieve this task in the future.

Finally, the same is to be said about other "magic" prescriptions for elimination of the deadly forms of social conflicts. Neither an establishment of the communistic, or socialistic, or capitalistic economies can accomplish this task because none of the historical societies with these types of economies has been free from this strife. No more hopeful are the beliefs in the establishment of a lasting international and internal peace by the means of a "massive retaliation" by nuclear or other "ultimate" instruments of warfare. Practiced for millennia, this policy of "peace through power" or through the Roman *si vis pacem para bellum* (if you want peace, prepare for war) has not given to humanity even modestly long periods of peace. Recent studies show that on the average the incidence of war occurred every two to four years in Greco-Roman and Euro-American history, while the incidence of an important internal disturbance took place about every five to seventeen years in these countries. Finally, the same studies disclose the fact that each time a more murderous means of warfare has been invented, the scale, the destructiveness, and the casualty of wars and revolutions have tended to increase instead of decreasing. These "sinister" facts sufficiently demonstrate the hopelessness of these policies for the realization of a lasting peace.

In summary, the unforgettable lesson from the catastrophe of this century convincingly shows that without increased "production, accumulation, and circulation" of the energy of unselfish love, no other means can prevent future suicidal wars, nor can they establish a harmonious order in the human universe. The mysterious forces of history seem to have given man an ultimatum: Perish by your own hands or rise to a higher moral level through the grace of creative love. This situation explains why a serious study of this energy is being started now, and why it is likely to become a most important field of research in the future.

2. The Manifoldness of Creative Love   "All this may be true," my skeptical friends often say to me, "but where are the proofs that this energy of love can work? And if so, how can we increase its production, accumulation, and circulation in the human world?" My answer to these difficult questions is as follows: Our extant knowledge of this energy is, so far, almost negligible. Our "know-how" of its efficient production and utilization is also very meager. And yet, this little knowledge and meager "know-how" warrant sufficiently the hypothesis that this "grace of love" is one of the three highest energies known to man (along with those of truth and beauty).

This energy or power is different from, and irreducible to the scalar quantities of physics called "force," "work," "power," and "energy." Its properties are qualitative rather than quantitative. As yet, we do not have any "unit" of this energy (like erg in physics) for its exact measurement. So far, we can only appraise very roughly when its (*a*) intensity, (*b*) extensity, (*c*) purity, (*d*) duration, and (*e*) adequacy are "notably greater or lesser." If these (*a, b, c, d, e*) are called "the dimensions of love," these "dimensions" are again different from the dimensions of "force" or "energy" in physics, expressed in the formulas: $ML_T{}^2$ and $ML^2{}_T{}^2$. We do not know, moreover, whether the law of conservation of energy and other principles of physics are applicable to the energy of love. The term "energy" is used here in its general meaning, as "ability to produce action or effect."

This energy of love appears to be an infinite universe which is inexhaustible qualitatively and quantitatively. It is like an iceberg: Only a small part of it is visible, empirically perceptible and observable. Of its many forms of being we can mention here its cosmic-ontological, biological, and psychosocial aspects.

Its Cosmic-Ontological Conception

In its cosmic-ontological aspect, altruistic love or Goodness, with Truth and Beauty, has been thought of as one of the three supreme forms of cosmic energy or reality or value operating not only in the human world but in the whole cosmos. Like the Christian Trinity—Father-Son-and Holy Ghost—Love-Truth-Beauty appear to be the highest values or energies inseparable but distinct from each other.

For this reason genuine truth is always good and beautiful, genuine beauty is invariably true and good, and genuine love is always true and beautiful. Potentially each of them contains the other two. In this trinity love is conceived as the unifying, integrating, and harmonizing cosmic power that counteracts the disintegrating forces of chaos, unites what is separated by enmity, builds what is destroyed by discord; creates and maintains the grand order in the whole universe. The familiar formula of practically all great religions "God is Love" and "Love is God," is one variation of this cosmic conception of unselfish love. The perennial cosmic struggle between Ahura-Mazda as the good cosmic Creator, in contrast to Ahriman as the wicked cosmic destroyer, in Zoroastrian religion; and generally, a good God as the benevolent creator in contrast to the evil Satan as the destroyer in many religions is another variation of this ontological conception of love. The Empedoclian theory that "all things coalesce into a unity in Love and they all separate in the enmity of Strife," developed by many subsequent thinkers, including F. Dostoevski, L. Tolstoi, V. Solovyev, and M. Gandhi, supplies a third variety of this ontological conception.

According to it, all empirical forms of unselfish love in the physical, biological, and human worlds are but the manifestations of this mysterious cosmic love.

Empirical Biological Altruism

As an empirical phenomenon, altruistic love means the specific behavior of living forms striving—instinctively or consciously—to be helpful to other organisms. In the plant-and-animal world it has mainly an instinctive-reflexological character. There it manifests itself in innumerable actions-reactions of cooperation and aid, as frequent and common, at least, as actions-reactions of the struggle for existence. Beginning with the reproduction activities of the unicellular and the multicellular organisms, and the actions involved in parental care for the helpless newborn progeny, and ending with thousands of diverse forms of rendering help, "the instinctive-reflexological altruism" among the animal and plant organisms proves itself to be at least as general and important a factor of their life and evolution as the factor of the struggle for existence. Without a minimum of aid and cooperation the very survival and continuation of practically all species are hardly possible. This is especially true of species like Homo sapiens whose babies are born helpless and require care for their survival for several months or years. In this sense cooperative, altruistic forces are biologically more important and vital than antagonizing forces. The balance between instinctive-reflexological altruistic tendencies and those which are inoperative and egoistic is relatively close among the organisms. All in all, however, group-centered, altruistic drives seem to be stronger than the drives of an egoistic nature.

Altruistic Love in the Human World: Its Psychological and Behavioral Characteristics

In the human world altruistic love appears simultaneously as a specific psychological experience, overt behavior, and social relationship. Despite a large variety of the concrete forms of altruistic experience, behavior, and relationship, all genuine altruistic experiences and actions have two common characteristics: First, the ego or "I" of the loving individual tends to merge and to identify itself with the loved "Thee"; second, all the loved individuals are regarded and treated as the end-value and not as a mere means for anything and anybody. The more genuine and pure the altruistic love the more conspicuous are these properties in it. In the experience and conduct of weak or pseudo-altruism, they tend to disappear.

Depending upon a different combination of emotional, volitional, and intellectual elements, altruistic love as a psychological experience has different "tonal qualities" or "colors." They are marked by such terms as empathy, sympathy, kindness, friendship, devotion, reverence, benevolence, admiration, respect, and others. All these forms are opposite to the forms of inimical psychological experience marked by such terms as hate, enmity, dislike, antipathy, envy, and the like.

If altruistic love remains in the state of a purely psychological experience and does not manifest itself in corresponding overt altruistic actions, then it becomes an "unfulfilled" or not "fully realized" love. Such a purely "psychological" or "ideological" or "speech-reactional" love often turns out to be pseudo-love or even "hypocritical altruism." The phenomena of this sort of "unfulfilled" love seem to be much more frequent in the human world than those of the "fulfilled," that is, "psychological" and "behavioral" love. There are millions of "ideological" or "speech-reactional" altruists in the human population; and there are comparatively few genuine "fulfilled" altruists who practice the noble altruistic precepts which they preach. As a social relationship love works in all interactions between two or more persons where one's valuable aims and real needs are shared and helped (to come about) by other persons. Accordingly, all interactions of this sort can be regarded as "workings" of love-energy in different degrees of purity, intensity, duration, and adequacy.

Altruistic and Sexual Love

If in sexual love the partners' egos are merged into one loving "we," and if the mates regard and treat each other as the end-value, then sexual love becomes one of the forms of altruistic love. When these characteristics are absent, and when sex-mates consider and treat each other as a mere means for obtaining pleasure or gratification, then sexual love turns into a relationship devoid of altruistic love. If sexual relations involve an element of coercion of one partner by the other (as in the case of rape, etc.), or an element of buying and selling services (as in the case of prostitution and "commercial" marriages), then sex-liaisons become a form of inimical relations opposite to altruistic love.

Five Dimensions of Altruistic Love

In order to be adequately described, and now and then roughly measured, the enormous complexity, multidimensionality, and quantitative-qualitative diversity of concrete phenomena of altruistic love can be reduced to five basic "dimensions" of intensity, extensity, duration, purity and adequacy of subjective altruistic purposes with their objective results.

(a) In intensity psychological-behavioral-social love ranges from zero to infinity, from a rich man's giving a few cents to the hungry, or a purely verbal highfalutin "love," up to a willing sacrifice of one's life—"body and soul"—for the well-being of the loved person. (b) In extensity love ranges from the zero point of love of oneself (egotism) up to the love of all mankind, all living creatures, and of the whole universe. (c) In duration altruistic love ranges from the shortest possible moment to years, decades, often throughout the whole life of an individual or of a group. (d) In purity love varies from the pure love motivated exclusively by love for love's sake, or by the love of a person for the person's sake, regardless of any utilitarian or hedonistic motives, down to the "soiled love" motivated by selfish expectations of advantage, utility, pleasure, or profit from such an "impure" love. Pure love knows no bargain, no reward. It asks nothing in return. Jesus' Sermon on the Mount and St. Paul's Epistle (I Corinthians 13) beautifully describe this sublime love. All forms of a "bargaining love," including heterosexual love in which the sex-partner is loved only because he or she gives pleasure or gratification, are examples of "impure" love. Sometimes such a love becomes devoid of altruistic elements and degenerates into a relationship of enmity and hate. (e) Adequacy of love fluctuates from "blind" to "wise" love. In inadequate love there is always a discrepancy between the subjective motives and purposes of love and the objective consequences of the unwise or inadequate actions through which love is realized. A mother may passionately love her child and may be ready to sacrifice anything for the child's welfare, but by realizing her love through wrong actions and means, she may spoil the child and endanger his well-being. All forms of such blind love are principally due to a lack of scientific knowledge as to what actions and means can or cannot produce the intended effects in the loved persons. Even the purest and most intense love can be blind if it manifests itself in scientifically wrong actions.

Such are the basic five "dimensions" of unselfish love. The higher any empirical love is on each and all of these dimensions, the greater it is quantitatively, and the more sublime qualitatively.

Altruistic Love as Eros and Agape

Some eminent religious, philosophical, and ethical thinkers conceive of altruistic love as ego-centered eros, while others view it as the egoless or the ego-transcending agape. The eros-conception of love assumes that a person who does not love himself or his own ego cannot love anyone else. Consequently, in order to be an altruist one does not need to transcend or annihilate his ego and his desire of good for the self. One needs only to be "enlightened" about one's real self-interests, to keep his or her ego from the excess of "unlightened selfishness," and to cooperate with other individuals for their mutual benefit. The ego-centered eros is thus utilitarian, hedonistic, and "rational" in its nature. It follows the following precepts: "live and let live," "help others in order to be helped by others," "do not harm others in order not to be harmed by others." Such an eros-love is discriminative: It is bestowed only upon those who deserve and reciprocate it. In contrast to eros agape-love is the egoless, self-giving love which "seeketh not its own" and freely spends itself. It possibly comes to mankind from above (from its cosmic source or God). Being inexhaustible in its richness, like the sun, agape shines upon and redeems the sinners no less than the virtuous. In this sense it is nondiscriminative, inscrutable, and incomprehensible to the ego-centered "rational" mind. The discriminative eros loves its object or person because of its or his virtue and value; the non-discriminative agape by its love creates value and virtue even in the hitherto valueless object or person. These two forms of unselfish love—and their mixed forms—have perennially operated in the life-history of mankind. Eros and the mixed form of love seem to have been more frequent and more common than agape-love. On the other hand, almost all of the greatest apostles of love, from Buddha and Jesus to Gandhi, have preached and practiced agape rather than eros. Perhaps this explains to some extent the gigantic influence of such apostles upon millions of individuals and upon the course of human history.

3. THE POWER OF UNSELFISH LOVE   Though the existing scientific knowledge about altruistic love is almost negligible, nevertheless, it can be reasonably contended that the energy of unselfish love potentially represents a gigantic creative, re-creative, and therapeutic power. When it is better understood, reverently treated, and wisely used, it can substantially help in freeing mankind from its gravest ills—war, crime, insanity, misery, and perversity.

For the last few decades, biology, psychology, sociology, and other branches of science have steadily converged toward these conclusions. Their rapidly increasing body of evidence convincingly demonstrates the creative and re-creative functions of love in the vital, mental, moral, and social life of individuals, societies, and mankind. Here are a few typical examples of many, well-ascertained, creative and therapeutic functions of unselfish love constantly performed in the human universe.

The Biological Functions of Love-Energy

The biological counterpart of love-energy manifests itself in the very nature and basic process of life. Often called "vital energy," it mysteriously unites various inorganic energies into a startling unity of a living unicellular or multicellular organism.

The Mysterious Energy of Love

This mysterious creation of living forms out of inorganic elements can be regarded as the first biological manifestation of the Empedoclean energy of love. The generation of practically all unicellular organisms from a parent cell, either by fission of the parent cell into four new individuals (zoospores) or into thirty-two or sixty-four microzooids with a subsequent conjugation of gametes into a new organism, is another manifestation of "biological love-energy"; "the two are for a time bound together in an interactive association," "the life of either one or the other is at some time dependent upon the potential or actual being of the other." Without such an interaction, without the parent cell supplying the vital tissues to the new organism, and without metabolic and physiological exchanges between parent and daughter cells, the appearance of a new organism as well as the very continuity of life itself becomes impossible. Cooperation of two organisms in sexual reproduction of multicellular organisms, accompanied by the passion of biological attraction between them, is a visible form of this "biological love" necessary for the maintenance of all such species and, through that, of life itself. The parental care of the offspring, during its period of helplessness, the care that in some species like Homo sapiens must last several years, is a still more explicit manifestation of biological love-energy. Without it such species would die out. A diverse cooperation and mutual aid functioning practically among all the species and necessary for their survival is a still more explicit and universal manifestation of biological love-energy. This cooperation, mutual aid, "gregarious or social instinct," "empathy," and "sympathy," are rightly considered a "fundamental characteristic of life-phenomena" as universal and basic as the trait of the "struggle for existence."

In short, without the operation of a biological counterpart of love-energy, life itself is not possible, nor its continuity, nor the preservation and survival of species, nor life evolution, nor the emergence and evolution of Homo sapiens.

Love and Suicide

The life-giving and life-sustaining power of love is strikingly demonstrated by the phenomena of suicide. We know now that the main cause of so-called "egoistic" and "anomic" suicide is the psychosocial isolation of the individual, his state of being lonely, not loving anyone and not being cared for by anyone. Whenever an individual's intimate attachments with other persons abruptly break down, when he becomes an unattached and disattached human atom in the universe, the chances of his committing suicide increase. When one's love and attachments to one's fellow men multiply and grow stronger, the chances of suicide decrease. For this reason the divorced, the widowed, and the single have a higher rate of suicide than the married, and among the married childless marriages yield a higher rate than the marriages with children. For the same reason atheists (unattached to any religious organization) are more frequently the victims of suicide than earnest believers; and among the believers the East-Orthodox, the Catholics, and the Jews have a lower rate than the more individualistic Protestants and free-thinkers (less closely bound together into one religious community). This shows that without a minimum of love, life tends to become a burden not worth living for the persons imprisoned within their egoistic shells.

Love and Longevity and Health

The energy of love shows its revitalizing qualities in many other forms. Other conditions being equal, of two persons with identical biological organisms, the kind and friendly person tends to live longer and to have better health than the unkind and especially the hate-possessed individual. Love in its various forms proves to be one of the most important factors of longevity and good health; being loved by others and loving others seems to be as important as any other single factor of vitality.

Important evidence for this is supplied by the life spans of Christian saints. An overwhelming majority of these saints were eminent altruists. My study of 3,090 Christian and Catholic saints and 415 Russian-Orthodox saints from the beginning of Christianity up to the present time has shown that they had longer life spans than their unsaintly and less altruistic contemporaries. Though the duration of life of thirty-seven per cent of these saints was cut off by premature death through martyrdom; though most of them lived an ascetic life, denying the satisfaction of many bodily needs; though many of them lived in non-hygienic conditions; and though the average life duration of the populations in the centuries before the nineteenth was notably lower than that of the United States population in 1920—in spite of all these adverse conditions the life duration of the saints as a group was somewhat higher than that of the American population in 1920.

The Curative Power of Love

That love has curative power is corroborated by a vast body of evidence which demonstrates healing power in regard to certain physical and mental disorders. Modern psychosomatic medicine correctly views strong emotional disturbances, especially of an aggressive, inimical, hateful, and antagonistic kind, as one of the basic factors of cardiovascular, respiratory, gastrointestinal, eliminative, skin, endocrinal, and genito-urinary disturbances, as well as of others such as epilepsy and headaches. The great anatomist, John Hunter, is reputed to have said concerning his angina pectoris, "My life is at the mercy of any rascal who can make me angry." Among other things, a strong, hateful, angry, inimical emotion robs one of peace of mind and through that (and other ways) undermines one's health and vitality. On the other hand, emotions of love, sympathy, and friendship tend to build one's peace of mind, one's equanimity toward such fellowmen and the world at large; for this and other reasons these emotions exert revitalizing and curative effects upon the organism and its disturbances.

For babies motherly love is a vital necessity. Deprived of warm love they sicken and die as quickly as they would sicken and die due to infection or hunger or improper diet. One of the latest studies along this line is by René A. Spitz. He reported and filmed the deaths of thirty-four foundlings in a foundling home. They had all the necessities and care except for motherly love in the foundling home. Its lack was sufficient to cause their deaths. The whole process of the withering of their vitality was filmed by Dr. Spitz, and can be seen and followed by the viewer. After three months of separation from their parents the babies lost their appetites, could not sleep, and became shrunken, while whimpering and trembling. After an additional two months they began to look like idiots. Twenty-seven foundlings died in their first year of life, seven in the second. Twenty-one lived longer, but "were so altered that thereafter they could be classified only as 'idiots'."

The therapeutic power of love is especially important in *preventing and healing mental and moral disturbances.* The grace of love—both in the forms of loving and being loved—is the most important condition for newly born babies to grow into morally and mentally sound human beings. Deprivation of love in childhood ordinarily leads such unfortunate persons to moral and mental disturbances.

In our age of psychoneuroses and of extensive juvenile delinquency, the Friends, the Mennonite, and the Hutterite communities in the United States yield either the lowest percentage of delinquents, criminals, and mentally sick persons or none. The main reason for this is that these communities try to practice, in the interrelationship of their members, the precepts of the Sermon on the Mount; they not only preach love but realize it in their daily behavior. No member of these communities is deprived of love and all are united into one real brotherhood.

The power of love, sympathy, empathy, and understanding

appears to be the main curative agent in diverse therapies of mental disorders. How curative the various psychiatric techniques actually are is exceedingly difficult to establish. The difficulties are due to a lack of objective criteria of improvement, diagnosis, record-keeping, etc. Various attempts to measure the curative effects of diverse psychiatric therapies give discrepant results from a very low percentage of patients, with temporary and slight improvement, up to some forty to sixty per cent of cases in psychoneurotic, sexual, and character disorders; and much lower percentages in epilepsy, migraines, stammering, chronic alcoholisms, and psychoses.

Regardless of the uncertainty and contrariety of the curative results of various psychiatric methods, on one vital point the psychiatrists seem to be in essential agreement, namely, that the main curative agent in all psychiatric techniques is the "acceptance" of the patient by the therapist, the rapport of empathy, sympathy, kindness, and love established between the therapist and the patient. In other words, the essence of curative therapy consists in the patient's exposure to the "radiation" of understanding, kindness, and love on the part of the therapist, instead of the atmosphere of rejection, enmity, reproof, and punishment in which the patient usually lives.

Summing up his study of the percentages and the degree of improvement of patients subjected to various psychiatric therapies, K. E. Appel concludes that "the therapeutic statistics appear to justify . . . that any therapy (in the sense of friendly rapport between the therapist and the patient) is in itself more fundamental than the type employed. There is something basically effective in the process of therapy in general which is independent of the methods employed."

The same conclusion is reached by F. E. Fiedler in his studies on the effectiveness of various psychiatric methods and especially of the "ideal therapeutic relationship." These studies show that, in spite of the wide differences in the theories and specific techniques of various psychiatric methods, the curative results of expert psychiatrists are fairly similar and that the eminent psychiatrists of different schools all agree on what is the best or the "ideal therapeutic relationship." It is marked by the following characteristics: complete empathy between the therapist and the patient, good rapport, and an atmosphere of mutual trust and confidence. The therapist sticks closely to the patient's problems; the patient feels free to say what he likes. The therapist accepts all feelings which the patient expresses as completely normal and understandable (according to the old precept "to understand all is to forgive all"). The patient assumes an active role in his own improvement. There is, in other words, a full understanding and sympathy between the parties involved in therapy.

In contrast to this ideal therapeutic relationship, the worst and least effective therapy is marked by a punitive therapist, who makes the patient feel rejected and little respected; by an impersonal, cold, often inimical relationship; by treatment of the patient as a child or an irresponsible, dangerous, stupid and inferior person.

C. R. Rogers describes the process of curing as follows:

> The client moves from the experiencing of himself as an unworthy, unacceptable, and unlovable person to the realization that he is accepted, respected, and loved, in this limited relationship with the therapist. Loved has here perhaps its deepest and most general meaning—that of being deeply understood and deeply accepted.

Similar is the conclusion of competent therapists in practically all the schools of psychiatry.

Since the real curative agent in mental disease is love in its various forms, many eminent apostles of love have been able to cure the mental disorders of legions of persons, although these altruists did not have any special psychiatric training. Their sublime love and supraconscious wisdom have been an excellent substitute for "little or no love" and for the professional training of ordinary psychiatrists. It is true that for the successful cure of especially serious mental disorders, a mere blind inadequate love, or too desiccated "intellectualized" love, is not enough.

Elsewhere it has been pointed out that truly creative and curative love must be not only pure and intensive, but also "adequate" or wise, choosing the adequate means for the realization of its supreme objective. Otherwise, it may miscarry and harm rather than benefit and cure. Though love seems to be the main curative agent in therapy, it must be adequate and wise love, guided by the supraconscious genius or scientific training of the therapist. The important need for adequate scientific training is not cancelled by the thesis that love is the main agent.

Love as a Vitamin of Children's Sound Growth

Love not only cures and revitalizes the individual's mind and organism but also proves itself to be the decisive factor of the vital, mental, moral, and social well-being and growth of an individual. Unwanted, unloved, rejected babies, deprived of the grace of love at an early age, tend to die or to grow into distorted "human vegetables." They are like seedlings planted in unfertile soil and deprived of the necessary ingredients for normal growth and activity. If in these conditions such seedlings do not die, they grow stunted, misshapen, weak, and ugly. Babies and children not blessed by the grace of love from their family, playmates, and neighbors grow into unhappy, defective, and often delinquent human beings. To love and be loved turns out to be the most important "vitamin" indispensable for the sound growth of an individual and for a happy course of life.

This is well corroborated by two opposite sets of evidence. On the one hand, children who are unloved, unwanted, and rejected by their parents, siblings, and others yield a much higher quota of juvenile delinquents, adult criminals, and otherwise physically and mentally defective persons than do children who are adequately loved by the members of their family, playmates, and others. Unloved and unloving children yield a higher proportion of warped, hostile, and unbalanced adults than do children blessed by the grace of love. The evidence supporting this generalization is substantial and adequate. On the other hand, almost all great altruists who quietly, without any tragedy or sudden conversion, grew into apostles of love came from harmonious families where they were wanted and loved.

These positive and negative sets of facts confirm the indispensable grace of love in forming a sound, integrated, and creative personality.

The total body of existing evidence, illustrated by the preceding samples, hardly leaves any doubt of the highly beneficial biological functions performed by the energy of love in human life and in the evolution of other species. Without this energy, the factor of the struggle for existence would have been entirely incapable of producing the evolution of living forms from the simplest unicellular organisms to Homo sapiens. Still less could it generate and maintain the very miracle of life itself and its creative transformations.

The Pacifying and Harmonizing Functions of Love

Besides biological functions, the energy of love serves mankind in many other ways. Thus, it has worked—and can increasingly do so—as the best "extinguisher" of interhuman aggression, enmity, and strife. The following actual case typically illustrates this role of love.

When an elderly Quaker lady entered her Paris hotel room she found a burglar rifling her bureau drawers where she had jewelry and money. He had a gun which he brandished. She talked to him quietly, told him to go ahead and help himself to anything she had. She even told him some places where there were valuables he had overlooked. Suddenly the man let out a low cry and ran from the room, taking nothing. The next day she received a letter from him in which he said: "I am not afraid of hate. But your kindness and love disarmed me."

Most of us have observed, and now and then have fruitfully used this "technique of sympathy and good deeds" to pacify our irritated children in their quarrels, to correct their misbehavior, to improve inimical relationships with our fellowmen. These observations and experiences convincingly testify that the words and actions of friendliness are quite often much more effective in stopping aggression and in transforming antagonistic relationships into amicable ones, than are threats, counter-aggression, hate, punishment, and other inimical actions-re-actions.

This conclusion is well confirmed by the experimental studies of the Harvard Research Center in Creative Altruism. For our experimental testing of this old truth, we took five pairs of students with a strong mutual dislike for each other. We set before them the task to change in three months, by the technique of "good deeds," their inimical relationships into amicable ones. We persuaded one partner of each pair to begin to render to the other partner small deeds of friendliness, like an invitation to lunch, to the movies, to a dance, or an offer to help with homework, and so on. At the beginning these deeds were performed without enthusiasm on the part of the renderer, and a few times were rejected by the other partner. However, being repeated, they began to melt enmity and eventually replaced it with warm friendship in four pairs and by "indifference" in the fifth pair. Similar experiments performed between mutually hostile nurses and patients in the Boston Psychopathic Hospital gave similar results.

Love Begets Love, Hate Begets Hate

The next evidence of the harmonizing power of love is supplied by innumerable facts showing that unselfish love is at least as "contagious" as hate and that love influences human behavior as tangibly as does hate. If and when an individual or group approach other persons or groups in a friendly manner, the respondents' answer in the overwhelming majority of cases to such an approach is usually pleasant. And the frequency of the friendly response to the friendly approach is at least as high as that of an inimical response to an aggressive approach.

Of numerous observations of this uniformity, only a few typical cases can be mentioned here. Dr. R. W. Hyde and H. Eichorn studied the approaches and responses of a group of patients at the Boston Psychopathic Hospital, and received the following results: to friendly approaches the respondents reacted in a friendly way in seventy-three per cent of actions-reactions; in sixteen per cent they responded in an aggressive manner; and in eleven per cent, in a neutral way. To aggressive approaches the respondents answered aggressively in sixty-nine per cent, friendly in twenty-five per cent, and indifferently in six per cent. The authors remark that the sixteen per cent of aggressive responses to friendly approaches is possibly due to the "super-ficiality of the friendly approach hiding an undercurrent of hostility or of disinterestedness." Likewise, a friendly response to the seemingly aggressive approach "may have been accepted by the recipients as compliments regarding their sexual po-tency." Whatever is the cause of the aggressive response to friendly approach and of the friendly response to the aggressive approach, the principle that love begets love and begets it as frequently as hate generates hate is clear from the data. The percentage of the friendly response to the friendly approach is even slightly higher than that of the unfriendly response to the unfriendly approach.

In my study of the relationship between each of 548 Harvard and Radcliffe students and his or her "best friend," the friend-ship was initiated in 23.7 per cent of cases by an action of kindness, help, sympathy, and care for one or for both parties; in the remaining 76.3 per cent of the cases it was due to desirable traits and to mutual supplementation of the values and experiences of the parties involved. There was not a single case of a friendship initiated by the aggression of one or of both parties. The inimical relationship between each of these students and his or her "worst enemy" started in 48.1 per cent of the cases by an action of aggression or unfriendliness on the part of one or of both parties involved. In the remaining 51.9 per cent of the cases the enmity was due to undesirable personal traits, to the incompatibility of the values, ideals, and aspirations of the parties involved. Here again friendliness tends to beget friendliness and aggression to generate enmity.

In another, more detailed investigation of how friendship started and developed with the "best friend" of each of seventy-three Harvard and Radcliffe students, and how the enmity with the "worst enemy" of each of these students grew, the results were fairly similar to the above: 24.2 per cent of the friendships were started by actions of kindness, generosity, help, sympathy of one or of both parties; 42.7 per cent of the enmities were started by aggressive and inimical actions of one or of both parties.

Here again the emergence and development of either friendship or animosity follows the formula: love begets love, enmity produces enmity.

In a large number of other investigations the rule of love begetting love has been well confirmed. The rule means that any genuine (and adequate) love or friendship effectively (though not always) changes the human mind and overt behavior in a friendly direction toward the friendly-acting person (s) . In this inner and overt transformation the power of love seems to be as effective as is the power of hate or animosity.

The Ennobling Power of Love

The power of love is further demonstrated by the numerous conversions of delinquent persons into honest ones, of ordinary sinful individuals into moral heroes and saints. A notable proportion of these real conversions has been started by acts of unexpected kindness or unmerited love toward the future convert, especially when he had reason to expect hate, anger, or retaliation on the part of the other party. The typical pattern of this kind of precipitation of altruistic and spiritual conversion is magnificently described by Victor Hugo in his *Les Misérables*. An ex-convict, Jean Valjean, bitter against the whole world, robs the good bishop who had given him hospitality. Caught with the goods on him, Jean Valjean is brought back to the bishop to certify that the goods were taken from him. The bishop's statement to the police that he has given these goods to Jean Valjean first dumbfounds the ex-convict and then shakes him to the bottom of his heart. This shock decisively turns the man to the path of subsequent transfiguration.

In various forms this kind of action frequently serves as a most powerful precipitating factor of moral ennoblement. Thus, among the saintly hermits we are told of several cases quite similar to that of Jean Valjean. The wisdom of the Desert Fathers generalized it in the form a rule: "It is not possible that by dint of harshness and austerity a man shall lightly be recalled from his [bad] intent: but by gentleness shalt thou call him back to thee." Jesus' "Love your enemy" and requite hatred with love; similar precepts of Taoism, Hinduism, Buddhism, and of most of the great religious and ethical systems, as well as the moral teachings of Tolstoi, Dostoevski, and Gandhi, are in fact among the most efficient, verified, and valid educational and therapeutic prescriptions. Of course, as any medicine, these precepts are not infallible; cases of failure of the rule are certainly known; but for the purposes of altruization it works much more frequently than the opposite rule of revenge, hateful retaliation, punishment, compulsion, anger, and animosity.

One of the poor patients of Dr. T. Haas (treated free of charge) stole his watch and then was caught. Dr. Haas informed the police that he had given the watch to the thief; then he invited the thief to visit him, talked to him cordially, and gave him money. The patient was radically cured of his antisocial tendencies.

From three to seven per cent of the living American Good Neighbors had their altruism precipitated by an unusual and unexpected kindness granted to them. Among Harvard and Radcliffe students 2.3 per cent were positively influenced by unexpected kindness. Two and nine-tenths per cent of seventy-three Boston converts were converted by the kindness of a believer in them. In thirty-seven per cent of the cases studied, gratitude is mentioned by Harvard and Radcliffe students as a factor in the awakening of religious and moral sentiments.

In contemporary psychotherapy, as we have seen, the techniques of kindness to the patient is a basic precept for every competent psychiatrist. Moreover, the technique of love is used in any successful moral and social education of normal children.

Use of the precipitant of kindness in spectacular and unspectacular form is a daily occurrence. Beginning with the daily altruization of members of all good families, where the technique of love and kindness is used as the principal attitude by members toward one another, and ending with hundreds of truly socializing interrelations between persons and groups, the therapy of overwhelming kindness has been one of the main forces maintaining the necessary minimum of justice, peace, harmony, and altruism in all societies and at all times.

Love as a Creative Power in Social Movements

With the exception of love as the mainspring of life and biological evolution, we have dealt so far mainly with the influence of love upon individuals and upon interindividual relationships. Fortunately, the power of love is not limited to this influence. It goes far beyond individual relationships and cases; it affects the whole social and cultural life of mankind. It operates as the driving force of man's creative progress toward ever-fuller truth, ever-nobler goodness, ever-purer beauty, ever-richer freedom, and ever-finer forms of social life and institutions. Throughout history each positive step in this direction has been inspired and "powered" by love, while any regressive step away from these values has been moved by hate.

Let us begin with a few cases of love's influence upon vast social movements. We can start with concrete questions: Can the nonviolent power of love stop war and ensure peace? Can the peaceful power of love achieve important social reforms and constructive changes? Can it compete with the social reconstructions inspired by hate and carried on by means of the violent and bloody struggle of clashing parties?

Love Can Stop War

A number of clear-cut historical events give an answer to these questions. As a first case of the power of love in regard to war and peace, Asoka's experiment can be mentioned. After his accession to the throne in 273 B.C. Asoka, like his predecessors, spent the first twelve years of his reign in wars for consolidation of his Indian empire. From Asoka's own inscriptions we learn that the horrors and miseries of wars aroused in him a deep remorse, a sense of most profound shame, and an understanding of the utter futility of war as a means of pacification and of social improvement. As a result, in 259 he entered a Buddhist order as a monk. This date marks the complete transformation of Asoka and of his policies. The successful emperor-warrior changed into a zealous apostle of peace, compassion, love, and good works. He began to preach, to practice, and to carry on "the policies of goodness, mercy, liberality, truthfulness, purity, and gentleness"—especially toward the conquered peoples—and the policies of liberation from "depravity, violence, cruelty, anger, conceit, and envy." By this policy he was able to secure peace for some seventy years. Considering that such a long period of peace occurred only three times in the whole history of Greece, Rome, and thirteen European countries, Asoka's achievement strongly suggests that the policy of real friendship can secure a lasting peace more successfully than the policy of hate and aggression unfortunately still followed by the governments of our time.

From the remotest past up to the present time this predatory policy of "peace through armed power," intimidation, coercion, and destruction has been followed by an overwhelming majority of governments in all countries. In spite of its past and present glorification, in spite of the endless repetition of this "enmity-fueled" policy, it has neither given lasting peace to humanity nor yielded even relatively long peaceful periods. After numberless applications of this predatory and hate-loaded policy for millennia, mankind of the twentieth century finds itself in the bloodiest, most militant, most inhuman, and most destructive century of the past twenty-five centuries.

The Fruitfulness of Love-Inspired Reconstruction

Asoka's policy was also highly successful internally. Without violence and bloodshed his reign fruitfully carried on one of the greatest reconstructions—vital, social, economic, political, legal, mental, moral, spiritual, and aesthetic—in the entire history of humanity. For its time and for all times, Asoka's reconstruction was deeper, greater, and broader than any reconstruction accomplished by means of bloody revolutions and violence. Again, the success of Asoka's internal policy was not accidental. It was a conspicuous case of a general rule that love-inspired reconstruction, aspiring to the real well-being of the people and carried out in a peaceful manner, is more successful and yields more lasting positive results than social reconstruction inspired by hate and carried out mainly by violence and bloodshed. Though in our age of violence and bloodshed this truth is entirely ignored, it still remains a valid truth. In addition to the peaceful reforms and bloody revolutions of the past, the events of our age also convincingly prove its validity. They prove it positively and negatively. The unlimited violence and the hate-inspired policies of World War I, of World War II, of the Korean War, and of the Chinese, the Russian, the Fascist, and the Hitler revolutions strikingly demonstrate the utter futility of hate-driven wars and revolutions in improving the total well-being of humanity.

The evidence of these wars and revolutions is confirmed also by the wars and revolutions of the past. Beginning with the oldest recorded Egyptian revolution (ca. 3000 B.C.) and ending with recent revolutions, all testify to the utter futility of hate-driven mass violence for realization of the well-being of mankind.

This negative evidence of war and revolution is confirmed, on the other hand, by the fruitfulness of peaceful and love-inspired orderly social reconstruction.

Striking historical examples of such reconstruction are supplied, first, by peaceful transformations of peoples, cultures, and social institutions by the founders, apostles, and early followers of religions and ethics of love, compassion, and mutual service. After all, Jesus, Buddha, Mahavira, Lao Tzu, Confucius, and Francis of Assisi had neither arms, nor physical force, nor wealth, nor any of the worldly means for exerting influence upon millions and for determining the historical destinies of nations and cultures. Nor to obtain their power did they appeal to hate, envy, greed, and other selfish lusts of human beings. Even their physical bodies were not those of heavyweight champions. And yet, together with a handful of followers, they reshaped the minds and behavior of untold millions, transformed cultures and social institutions, and decisively conditioned the course of history. None of the greatest conquerors and revolutionary leaders can even remotely compete with these apostles of love in the magnitude and durability of the change brought about by their activities. Even more important, the great apostles of love succeeded in working out the gigantic and imperishable change in the "upgrade" direction of creative love instead of the much easier "downgrade" direction of hate and bloody struggle.

If for a moment we imagine Christianity removed from the historical life, social institutions, and culture of the West; Confucianism, Taoism, and Buddhism from the life and culture of China; Hinduism, Buddhism, and Jainism from the sociocultural universe of India—only a chaotic mass of debris remains from the culture, social institutions, and historical life of these countries. Without their ethico-religious systems the whole history of these countries becomes incomprehensible.

Likewise, without the gigantic stream of sublime love poured into it by the apostles of love, the life of humanity would have been sorely lacking in the very minimum of moral foundation necessary for its existence and survival. *Bellum omnium contra omnes* (war of everyone against everyone) and suicidal mutual extermination would have been the lot of humanity had this sublime love been absent.

And how, by what force, have these moral leaders been able to exert this tremendous influence? Only through the grace of the sublime love they were blessed with and through wisdom of the love they discovered and opened to their fellowmen. As mentioned, they did not command any armed force or machinery of state organization; nor did they possess wealth and its attendants; they were not great intellectual scientists nor master artists. Their only weapon was the mysterious power of love. For this reason their influence stands as an indisputable demonstration of the virtually unlimited power of love. By this power they ennobled, maintained, and recreated the biological, social, and cultural life of mankind. By this power they counteracted and limited the destructive influence of the forces of strife—and are doing so up to the present moment.

This power of love is not responsible for the bloody movements and deeds often perpetrated in the name of Jesus, Buddha, or other geniuses of creative love. Religious wars and persecution, religious political machines and their great inquisitors have nothing to do with the teachings and activities of the great apostles of love. If anything, these machines, bureaucratic inquisitors, wars, persecution, intolerance, and hypocrisy are the negation and perversion of the power of love by the founders of the great religions of love. The militant activities of these machines are mainly the manifestations of the forces of ego-centered domination and not of the forces of love.

The recent reorganization of India can serve as a modern example of the reconstruction inspired and "fueled" by the power of love. It was started and has been carried on under the leadership of Gandhi and his co-workers. Their policy has been motivated by creative love at its purest and best. Hate and enmity have been explicitly ruled out from their movement—so also have violent means and methods. Throughout its whole history the Gandhi-led movement was peaceful and orderly, and its constructive results have been truly astounding. It achieved complete political independence for India's four hundred million people. This result alone exceeds the political achievements of practically any violent revolution known in human history. Gandhi's movement succeeded in the liberation and equalization of some sixty million outcasts in India—another result hardly rivaled by the "liberation" of any violent revolution. Besides the inestimably fruitful reconstruction of India, it has produced gigantic reverberations in the entire human universe.

This power of love continues to work in India, in the activities of one of the disciples of Gandhi, "The holy man" Acharya Vinola Bhave. Practicing the principles of love he preaches, this gentle ascetic—by merely appealing to the goodness of human nature—has already achieved astounding results in his "one-man crusade."

The fruitfulness of social reforms inspired by love rather than by hate is demonstrated by practically all such reconstructions in the history of various countries. The "Great Reforms" of 1861-65 in Russia that liberated serfs and basically reorganized political, social, economic, and cultural institutions is another highly successful peaceful reconstruction. The westernization of Japan and the basic reorganization of its institutions, carried on in orderly fashion during the second half of the nineteenth century and the beginning of the twentieth, is another successful reconstruction. Its positive success becomes especially clear when it is contrasted with Japan's violent experiments to reconstruct herself and Asia as the "co-prosperity sphere." Starting with the Pearl Harbor attack, this "reconstruction," carried on by means of unlimited bloodshed, resulted in the catastrophic defeat of Japan and in a deadly devastation of China and other Asiatic countries. This shows indeed that "it does not pay" to be violent and destructive.

If something good comes from wars and bloody revolutions, it is due to a current of unselfish love and disinterested desire to help the suffering multitudes, the aftermath of most wars and great revolutions. Otherwise, most of the positive results of such violent movements are obtained through spoliation of some other groups, at the cost of their suffering, of their well-being, and often of their very life. Most of the "achievements" of wars and revolutions are gained by the plundering of the defeated party by the victorious group.

While the victorious ruling faction profits by war or violent revolution, the bulk of the populations of both struggling parties must bear the cost. And the bloodier the struggle, the greater the cost—in life, property, and happiness—for the large masses. In protracted and bloody struggles, the vital, economic, mental, and moral losses of the vast strata of both parties ordinarily far exceed their gains. While the small ruling groups of Genghis Khan or Napoleon, of Marius or Sulla, of Caesar or Antony, of Cromwell or Robespierre, of Lenin or Hitler for a short time enormously profited by their victories, the vast multitudes of their peoples were almost ruined by the struggle. Sometimes the ruin was irreparable and eventually led to the decline of the "bled" nations and their cultural creativity. Bloody civil strife

[189]

and the Peloponnesian War ushered in the decay of Greece; the costly wars and civil struggles of Marius and Sulla, of the First and Second Triumvirate, started the decline of the Roman Empire. The bloodshed of the French Revolution and of the Napoleonic Wars prepared the subsequent eclipse of France. The same can be said of the wars of Suleiman the Magnificent in regard to the Turkish Empire, or of the decay of the Old Kingdom, of the Middle and the New Empire in Egypt. Finally, the bloodiest revolutions and the world wars of our time have brought the whole of mankind, especially the belligerent and turbulent West (including Russia) to the brink of an apocalyptic catastrophe. Hate-inspired butcheries do not improve social well-being, nor do they cure social illness. Only wisely guided forces of love and free cooperation can perform these functions.

Love Terminates Catastrophes

Generally, the pacifying power of love appears to be the main force which terminates long and mortally dangerous catastrophes in the life of nations. A systematic study of all such catastrophes in the history of ancient Egypt, Babylonia, China, India, Persia, Israel, Greece, Rome, and of the Western countries uniformly shows that all such catastrophes were finally overcome by an altruistic ennoblement of the people, culture, and social institutions of these nations. This ennoblement often emerges and spreads in the form of a new religion of love and compassion (like Buddhism or Jainism or Christianity), or as moral and spiritual enrichment of the old religion and its moral commandments. We must not forget that practically all the great religions emerged in catastrophic circumstances and, during their initial period, were first of all and most of all moral social movements inspired by sympathy, compassion, and the Gospel of Love. They set out to achieve the moral regeneration of a demoralized society. Only later on did such movements become burdened by complex theological dogmas and impressive rituals. This is equally true of the emergence and initial period of Confucianism, Taoism, Zoroastrianism, Hinduism, Jainism, Buddhism, Mosaic and Prophetic Judaism, Christianity, and other ethicoreligious movements.*

Love Increases the Life-Span of Societies

Love-energy not only increases the longevity of individuals, but also the life-span of societies and organizations. Social organizations built mainly by hate, conquest, and coercion, like the empires of Alexander the Great, Caesar, Ghengis Khan, Tamerlane, Napoleon, or Hitler, have had, as a rule, a very short life—a few years, decades, rarely a few centuries. So it has been with various organizations in which unselfish love plays an unimportant role. Thus the average longevity of small economic establishments like drug, hardware, or grocery stores in this country is only about four years. Big business firms (listed on American and European stock exchanges) survive on the average only about twenty-nine years. Even the longevity of most of the states rarely goes beyond one or two centuries. The longest existing organizations are the great ethico-religious bodies like Taoism, Confucianism, Hinduism, Buddhism, Judaism, Jainism, Christianity, and Mohammedanism. All of these organizations have already lived for more than one thousand years—some for over two thousand—and there are no clear signs of their dissolution in the foreseeable future. The secret of their longevity probably lies in their dedication to the altruistic education of mankind and, generally, to the cultivation of love in the human universe.

4. LOVE AS THE SUPREME FORM OF HUMAN RELATIONSHIP

It goes without saying that the finest, the noblest, and the happiest human society is the society of individuals bound together by a love relationship. This is the freest society, because

* See P. Sorokin, *Man and Society in Calamity*, chs. X, XI, XII.

the very meaning of "I love to be here," or "I love to do this," or "I love to be a member" is the highest expression of the free desire, action, and preference of a person. It is the happiest society because loving and being loved is the highest form of happiness in human relations. It is the most peaceful and harmonious society; it is also the most creative, most beautiful, and noblest.

Not only the love relationship is the best, but its minimum is absolutely necessary for a long and enjoyable existence of human society and social life generally. A society bound together only by coercive bonds is but the worst "prison." Prisoners always try to escape from it. It is a social hell hardly worth living in. If mankind were destined to live in such a universal prison, neither mankind nor its social life could survive. Plato and Aristotle were quite right in their statement that true friendship or love is the most vital stuff of all true social relationships.

5. LOVE POWER IN KNOWLEDGE, BEAUTY, GOODNESS, FREEDOM, AND HAPPINESS   Finally, love furnishes considerable driving force to the total power of each of the highest values of human life; to the power of truth and knowledge, of beauty and freedom, of goodness and happiness. Thus *love of truth* makes the search for truth more forceful, enjoyable and indefatigable than the pursuit of truth either coercively imposed or contractually stipulated. Most of the valid truths of humanity have been discovered through the love of truth rather than through coercion or obligation. The love of truth not only stimulates scientific discoveries, inventions, philosophical and religious verities, but also directly contributes to our knowledge and learning. Through empathy, communion, and participation in the experience of all who are loved, love enormously enriches our poor individual experience. This empathic, sympathetic, loving way of learning is possibly one of the surest and most efficient methods of cognition and is the most fruitful way to truth and knowledge. Love, then, transforms itself into truth and knowl-

edge. In these two ways the power of love greatly reinforces the power of truth and knowledge.

Similarly love greatly increases the power of beauty. In a sense love is beauty's indispensable component. Anything that one loves and looks at through loving eyes becomes "lovely," that is, beautiful. Anything unloved appears "unlovely," often ugly. Since the love experience is beautiful in its very nature, everything that love touches becomes beautiful. Love generates the search for beauty and supplies an immense driving power to the energy of beauty itself. Through the factor of beauty, love notably affects our life and the course of history. Love power has been working in and is embodied in all the fine arts phenomena, beginning with the enjoyment of a sunset and the beauty of the beloved and ending with Homer's epic poems, Shakespeare's tragedies, Beethoven's and Bach's music, Michelangelo's sculpture, and all great paintings and architecture.

Likewise, love for freedom has been instrumental in all movements for the realization of freedom in human history. Even more, love experience is freedom at its loftiest and best. To love anything is to act freely, without compulsion or artificial stimulation. To be free means to do what one loves to do. In this sense, love and true freedom are synonymous. Compulsion is the negation of love. Where there is love there is no coercion; where there is coercion there is no love. And the greater the love the greater the freedom. Without love, all the Bills of Rights and all the constitutional guarantees of freedom are but empty shells.

There is no need to argue that love is the heart and soul of ethical goodness itself and all great religions. Their central command has always been love of God and of thy neighbor. Their main verity is "God is Love and Love is God." Without love there is no morality and no religion. If the stream of love in religion or ethics dries up, both become empty and dead.

Finally, love experience is the supreme form of happiness. Love "beareth all things . . . never faileth." Love does not fear anything or anybody. When love is unbounded and pure, it is "the peace of God that passeth all understanding."

Each experience of loving and being loved, however simple and impure, is already a happy experience, "a moment of sunshine" in our grayish life process. An experience of a great love is the highest bliss of human life. And vice versa. Any life deprived of love is a mere miserable existence. Such a life often becomes unbearable and leads its victims to suicide.

Thus the power of love generates, inspires, reinforces, and operates in all the individual and collective actions of the realization of truth and knowledge, of goodness and justice, of beauty and freedom, or the *summum bonum* and happiness, throughout the whole creative history of humanity. When all the manifestations of love power are rightly understood, one can but agree with Gandhi's and Dostoevski's restatements of the old truth on the power of love. Dostoevski wisely counsels: "Love all God's creation, the whole and every grain of sand in it. Love every leaf, every ray of God's light. Love the animals, love the plants. Love everything. If you love everything, you will perceive the divine mystery in things. Once you perceive it, you will begin to comprehend it better every day, and you will come at last to love the whole world with an all-embracing love. . . . Seeing the sins of men, one sometimes wonders whether one should react to them by force or by humble love. Always decide to fight them by humble love. If it is carried through, the whole world can be conquered. Humble love is the most effective force, the most terrific, the most powerful, unequaled by any other force in the world."

The Production of Love Energy

6. THE PRODUCTION, ACCUMULATION AND DISTRIBUTION OF LOVE ENERGY If the altruistic transformation of man and man's universe is the paramount item on today's agenda of history, and if creative, unselfish love is one of the highest energies known,

this means that at this juncture of history the greatest task of mankind consists of increasing the production, accumulation, and eventual use of this energy. Like food, heat, electricity and other forms of energy, love-energy does not grow by itself: in some way it has to be produced or, at least, collected and stored from "natural" sources, in order that all living societies can have their minimum portion. For without minimum cooperation, good will, and mutual aid, no society can survive even for a few days or weeks or months; it would suffer immediately from incessant tensions, conflicts, and "civil wars." No order, no security, and no peaceful work of procuring even the means of subsistence are possible in a society of human beasts motivated only by selfish lusts, hate, and greed unchecked by the energy of love.

The main difference between the production of love and of other more tangible energies is that in technologically advanced societies an enormous amount of time, means, and collective effort are devoted to the organized production of physical energies, based on the knowledge of physical, chemical, and biological phenomena. In contrast to this, contemporary technology of love production in practically all societies is given little thought, time, or effort; it still remains in the most rudimentary form, corresponding to the primitive manual technology of material production in preliterate tribes. We "collect" and use love energy only insofar as it is "naturally" produced in our societies.

The time has come for humanity not only to begin to understand the nature, the forms, and the how and why of love, but also to endeavor to design more efficient techniques for its production. We already understand that the "love commodity" is the most necessary commodity for any society; that without its minimum no other commodities can be obtained in abundance; and that at the present time it is a commodity on which depends the very life and death of humanity.

Here, then, is the briefest summary of the essentials of where, how and by what means the production of love energy goes on at the present.

(*a*) Love, in all its forms, is produced by the interaction of human beings. Any action of love, rendered by *A* to *B*, or mutually, or any love reaction of *A* to *B*'s aggressive, offensive, hateful action would be a generation of love energy in human interaction.

The more intense, extensive, durable, pure, and adequate the love that pulsates in such actions is, and the more numerous the actions are, the greater the love production in these interactive ("fission") processes.

(*b*) Love is produced in these interactions for the most part haphazardly, along with hate and its varieties. There are hardly any safeguards or precautionary measures to prevent the production of hate instead of love in these interactions.

(*c*) In all these interactions the production of love for the most part proceeds "spontaneously" and "naturally," without special aims, devices, tools, or techniques to organize production on a more efficient level in order to produce a greater quantity and a better quality of love energy for the group and for humanity.

(*d*) Only a few persons and agencies—"the inventors and engineers of love-production"—have purposefully endeavored to improve in their own interactions this process of love production, or have devoted themselves to this task to a considerable degree. The following are examples of these "inventors and engineers."

(1.) All the great apostles of love and the moral educators of humanity: Christ, Buddha, St. Francis of Assisi, Gandhi, and the many less important "producers of love," kind and good neighbors, and all who habitually perform unselfish acts of love.

(2.) Many great religious educators. One of the central values of their religion has been the ethical or moral code of love, whether in the form of "love your enemy" and other moral precepts of Taoism; or the "reverence, benevolence, and reciprocity" of Confucianism; or the "compassion and love" of Hinduism, Buddhism, and Jainism; or the Ten Commandments of Judaism; or the commandments of "Mercy, Compassion, and Love" of Mohammedanism; or the sublimest norms of the Sermon on the Mount in Christianity.

(3.) All great and small creators in the field of constructive truth (science, philosophy, scientific technology) and of real beauty (all the fine arts). As I have indicated, these values are transformable to a degree into the values of goodness and love; all those who have enriched humanity with truth and beauty have also contributed to a more efficient production of love.

(e) Besides these kinds of individuals, a few social groups or institutions have contributed a great deal to the production of love and to its improvement. Such groups or institutions are similar to small workshops and farms for the production of the material necessities in agricultural and manufacturing (not machinofacturing) societies. Among such agencies the family has been the most important. Like a workshop producing for a local market, the family production of love has also been limited to the members of the family. Only indirectly and occasionally has the family produced love that extended beyond it for the human "world market."

Other love-producing groups are: groups of close friends; religious groups that earnestly seek to promote altruistic relationships among their members and partly with outsiders; small local communities, schools, and educational institutions; occupational unions, castes, and orders; and other manibonded groups. To a degree, each group that has solidarity among its members generates a certain amount of love. Most groups, however, tend to generate a relatively weak, impure, short-lived, unextensive, and inadequate current of love. And besides, such love tends to circulate mainly or exclusively among the members of the group, often followed by the generation of hate and animosity toward some common enemy or by their common exploitation of outsiders for the benefit of the group. As a result some groups produce more hate than love and solidarity. All this shows the astounding lack of organized effort for an abundant production of love energy. At present this neglect threatens the very future of humanity. Hence the imperative need for a decisive improvement in the production of love. The following steps can help in this task.

A. *The Increase of Creative Heroes of Love*

The first step toward a greater output of a better quality of love is to increase the exceptional apostles of love among us. The total influence of the heroes of love, of science, of beauty, of religion, far transcends their direct, face-to-face influence. Just as the aesthetic and other effects of the works of Homer, of Shakespeare, of Bach or Beethoven, of Plato or Newton have affected millions of human beings, so the total effect of the lives and activities of the great altruists like Buddha, Jesus, St. Francis, and Gandhi has been almost infinite, both for the production of love and for the enrichment of humanity. For centuries and millennia this energy has incessantly issued from these "fountainheads of love," has spread among millions, has permeated social institutions and cultures, and has maintained the necessary minimum of solidarity in groups. Even the deaths of these heroes of love have not stopped the process of love generation started during their lives: After their deaths Buddha and Jesus possibly radiated more love than they did during their lifetimes. This means that love energy is as imperishable as any other form of energy.

These observations show that an increase in the number of heroes of love means an increase of love output far beyond a mere numerical increase of altruistic persons.

Herein lies the enormous significance of such heroes of love. Their outward appearance changes from period to period, from society to society. Now they appear as religious leaders; now as pious nobles; now as hermits; now as monks; now as social reformers; now as just good neighbors or as housewives and husbands. Their external garb changes, but their real function remains the same: They act as power stations generating the energy of love for humanity.

B. *The Increase of Creative Heroes of Truth and Beauty*

Each great creator in the fields of science, philosophy, religion, technology, or the fine arts is also a gigantic power station generating the energies of truth and beauty. So far as these energies are transformable into the energy of love (and vice versa), an increase in the number of these heroes of truth and beauty leads indirectly to an increase in the production of love (and vice versa). Therefore all measures that facilitate an increase of *constructive* creativity in the fields of truth and beauty also serve the purpose of increasing creativity in the field of goodness.

C. *The Increase of Love Production by the Rank and File*

However important, an increase in the production of love by the heroes of goodness, truth, and beauty is not enough. It must be paralleled by at least a modest increase in love generation by ordinary persons and groups. If the mass of ordinary mortals would simply abstain from murdering other human beings; if they would cut in half their daily actions of hate and would double their daily good deeds, such a modest improvement in their moral conduct would enormously increase the output of love and decrease the output of hate, and thereby the general ethical and social level of humanity would be raised to a much higher level. This modest elevation of the ethical behavior of mortals would be quite sufficient to prevent new catastrophic wars, and would improve enormously the social harmony of humanity.

D. *An Increase in the Production of Love by Groups and Institutions*

An increase in love production by the rank and file is possible only when an increase occurs also in the groups or institutions to which they belong. As a rule, the altruization of an individual is possible only through the altruization of his groups or institutions; and vice versa, the altruization of institutions or groups is possible only through that of their members.

If within each group the love relationship among its members grows, the production of love by the group and by its members increases. Up to the present time an increased generation of love within a group has often been followed by an increase of discrimination and antagonism toward outside groups and persons. This has tended to cancel the increase of love generation within the group. As a result, humanity as a whole has profited little from this double process of an increase of love generation within a group followed by an increase of hate output toward the outside world.

This mutually cancelling process is senseless; it must be replaced by an increase of love within each group without an increase of antagonism toward the outside world. It is indeed possible to increase the love of the members of a family or group toward one another without increasing antagonistic discrimination against the rest of the human universe. When such a change is made, an increase in the love generation of each group will lead to an increase in the total output of all humanity.

E. *The Increase of Love-Production by the Total Culture*

Finally, all cultural systems of science, philosophy, religion, ethics, law, fine arts, humanistic and social disciplines, as well as applied technology in all fields of human activity, must be permeated by the grace of love and freed from the poison of hate to a much greater degree than they have been up to the present time.

Contemporary science serves not only the God of Love, but also the Satan of hate and destruction. Contemporary philosophy and pseudo-religion have upon human beings not only morally ennobling and loving effects, but to a hardly less degree the opposite effects of hate and strife. This is still more true of most of the contemporary fine arts: literature, music, painting, sculpture, and drama. It also applies to contemporary law and pseudo-ethics, social theories, and humanistic ideologies, not to mention contemporary "technology" of the physical, biological, and social sciences. They all play a double role in their influence on individuals and groups. In one role they generate love, make human beings ethically nobler and more creative, and integrate them into one human family of mutually respecting and loving members. In the other role they radiate hate and discord, demoralize and debase ethically, disintegrate intellectually, and destroy and kill.

If we need to increase the love output of humanity, then all the main cultural systems must evidently be so reconstructed as to radiate only the positive love rays and cease to generate the negative hate rays. This double radiation has been one of the principal reasons why the positive effects have been largely canceled out by the negative ones, and why, as a net result, all the enormous progress of scientific discovery, technological invention, philosophy, the fine arts and other cultural systems has not resulted in a decrease of hate and interhuman warfare. Twentieth-century humanity cannot boast of being better morally than the humanity of the Stone Age. If we can reconstruct these cultural systems so as to eliminate their hate generation, we shall incalculably increase the love production of all humanity.

F. *Summary*

Through these five steps the production of love in humanity can be increased and the generation of hate can be decreased enormously. The total result will be an amount of love-energy quite sufficient to prevent bloody strife or enmity on a large scale and to build a harmonious human order, far nobler and happier than any hitherto known. If and when humanity or its leaders earnestly decide to carry it out, they will discover that the plan is quite realizable and not merely a utopian dream.

7. THE ACCUMULATION AND DISTRIBUTION OF LOVE-ENERGY

Like other forms of energy, love-energy can also be accumulated or stored (a) in individuals, (b) in social institutions, and (c) in culture. The storing of love energy in individuals means making their love actions and reactions spontaneously habitual, interiorized, and rooted to such an extent that they become second nature. If the habituation is begun during earliest childhood and continuously practiced thereafter, it will indeed amount to a great accumulation of love-energy in individuals and through them in humanity as a whole.

The storing of love energy in social institutions (or organized groups) and in culture will be achieved through the permeation of cultural systems and institutions—their structures and functions, their agencies and vehicles—with the grace of love energy. Constructed and reorganized in conformity with the principles of love, these cultural systems and social institutions would become a multitude of gigantic power systems, incessantly generating love, storing it, and radiating it upon all human beings. In the gentlest but most effective way, love, radiated by culture and by social institutions, would create a permanent atmosphere that would pervade all human beings from the cradle to the grave. Its total amount, stored in individuals, institutions, and culture can be sufficient for the practical purposes of humanity; (a) for the prevention and elimination of crime, revolutions, wars, and other forms of conflict where there is underlying hate, envy, and unhappiness; (b) for the maintenance and growth of man's creative activity; (c) for decreasing and eventually eliminating the worst forms of suffering, unhappiness, loneliness, illness, and unnecessary death; (*d*) for making the whole world a friendly, warm, and inspiring cosmos for everyone.

Like other forms of energy, accumulated love can also be distributed according to the particular needs of various persons and groups. When an urgent need arises, demanding the release of an unusually intense or large amount of love-energy—when a catastrophe or dreadful conflict impends or a conflagration of hate needs to be extinguished—its accumulation would make possible such a release.

Through various general and special agents, friends, neighbors, and through special channels for its circulation, love-energy can be directed to those groups or persons who at any given moment need it most. An individual struck by a great tragedy can best be consoled by the intensive love focused on him by his closest friends, neighbors, and large groups. A person or group afflicted by the disease of hate, mental depression, or suicidal tendencies can often be cured by a concentrated love that understands, forgives, and cures. In these and thousands of similar cases, love-energy can be poured on the person, the group, or the danger spot in such abundance and intensity that the threatening conflagration is extinguished, hate epidemics are cured, catastrophe is averted. Life again becomes worth living for the afflicted persons and groups, and the world once more appears as a sunny and warm marvel.

Again it should be noted that this whole matter of production, accumulation and distribution of love is realizable and not utopian.

8. THE TECHNIQUES OF ALTRUISTIC TRANSFORMATION   The outlined tasks of moral transformation of mankind can be notably helped by recourse to several efficient techniques for production and accumulation of love-energy. Despite our meager knowledge of them, some thirty techniques are known to exist. With increased research our understanding of them may deepen and new ones may be invented. The known techniques range

widely in complexity from the crudest to the most subtle. As examples of the simpler techniques can be mentioned the use of various chemical, physical, and biotic agents; training in posture and control of the automatic nervous system; and techniques of conditioned reflexes, habit formation, mechanical drilling, and punishment and reward. More refined methods involve rational persuasion and scientific demonstration, reinforced by mobilization of man's emotional, effective, and volitional forces; use of the heroic examples; direct life experience; and the inspiration of the fine arts. The subtle techniques to increase the altruism of man include stimulation of man's creativity; concentration, meditation, and self-examination; and especially the complex methods of the Yogas, of Zen Buddhism, Sufism, of somatophysic techniques of orthodox Christianity, and the techniques invented by the founders of religions of love and of the great monastic orders (St. Basil the Great, St. Benedict, St. Francis of Assisi, St. Bernard, St. John Climacus, John Cassian, St. Francois de Sales, Ignatius Loyola, and others). The inventors of these techniques knew a great deal about the effective procedures for man's moral transformation; otherwise they could not have become successful moral educators of humanity.

Three Types of Altruistic Transformation

A careful study of the process of altruization of the great apostles of unselfish love shows at least three different ways of becoming such an apostle and, respectively, three types of altruists: (*a*) "fortunate" altruists who from their early childhood display a very humble ego, a well-integrated set of moral values, and well-selected social affiliations with good persons and groups—their ego, values, and affiliations all centered around the values of love, the supreme "self," or God. Like grass, quietly and gracefully they grow in their altruistic creativity without any crisis, catastrophe, or painful conversion. A. Schweitzer, John Woolman, Dr. T. Haas, and many others exemplify this type; (*b*) "catastrophic" and "late" altruists whose life is sharply divided into two periods: pre-altruistic, preceding their transformation, and altruistic, following the total transformation of their personality, prepared by a disintegration of their selfish ego, values, and group affiliations and precipitated by catastrophies (sickness, death of beloved, etc.), and other events in their lives. The process of transformation of such persons is ordinarily very difficult and painful and it lasts from a few months to several years. During this agonizing period the respective persons have to perform the difficult operation of a basic rearrangement of their ego, values, and group affiliations, subordinating these to, and centering them around, the supreme value of love. When this operation is completed and well interiorized, a new altruistic personality emerges and grows up to the end of its life. Buddha, St. Francis of Assisi, Brother Joseph, Ignatius Loyola, St. Augustine, St. Paul, and others exemplify this type; (*c*) finally, the intermediary type is marked by some of the traits of the fortunate and the late-catastrophic types. St. Theodosius, St. Basil the Great, M. Gandhi, St. Theresa, Sri Ramakrishna, and others are examples of this type.

The main factor of the differences between the ways of the fortunate and the late catastrophic altruists seems to be the kind of family from which these two types of altruists have come and the kind of groups with which they were associated in their childhood. The overwhelming majority of the fortunate altruists have come from harmonious families permeated by warm and wise love, devotion, and respect of its members for each other. In addition to the happy family, some of the fortunate altruists in their childhood were affiliated with orderly and kind persons, neighborly groups, and wise leaders. In the family as well as in the neighborly groups they received an abundance of love, a sound set of values, and a deeply grounded moral discipline. Their infancy being molded in this way, they could quietly grow in their altruism without any crisis or conversion.

In contrast to the fortunate way of altruistic growth, the majority of the catastrophic altruists came from disharmonious families, broken homes, and neighborhoods deficient in love, wisdom, and discipline. In their infancy and childhood they did not have a real opportunity to be well integrated—morally, mentally, and socially. For this reason, later on they could not become altruistic without a painful crisis and catastrophic conversion.

The fortunate, the catastrophic, and the intermediary ways of altruistic transformation have been and are operating also in the altruistic changes of the ordinary rank and file. Those of our fellowmen and women who since their infancy were endowed by their family and other groups with a loving heart, sound mind, and wise discipline do grow quietly and gracefully in creative love. Without crises and conversions they progress in their moral ennoblement. Those of our contemporaries who did not have the fortune of being born and reared in a happy family, neighborhood, and environment are becoming morally ennobled, mainly via the hard way of the catastrophic altruists. Their altruistic transformation is much more difficult and ordinarily less successful than that of the incipient "fortunate altruists." For a moral conversion of this type of person the finest and most delicate techniques of altruization are often insufficient: Frequently, painful crises, frustrations, and catastrophes, or the harsher techniques of a coercive nature, are necessary to start their process of conversion. Taken alone, these harsh stimuli rarely produce moral ennoblement. Quite often they instead create demoralization. However, when applied together with the refined techniques of altruization, and in a proper historical situation, they become "the precipitating factors" of the moral transformation of many catastrophic altruists.

Finally, many of us follow the path of the "intermediary" altruists in our pilgrimage toward moral improvement. In these three ways a considerable part of today's humanity moves toward the "positive moral polarization" necessary to oppose the destructive process of demoralization or "the negative polarization" of another part of humanity.

The Law of Polarization

In order to understand these last few statements a few words about the law of religious and moral polarization in the times of catastrophes are advisable. Contrary to the Freudian claim that calamity and frustration uniformly generate aggression; and contrary to the old claim, reiterated recently by Toynbee, that we learn by suffering, and that frustration and catastrophes lead uniformly to the moral and spiritual ennoblement of human beings, the law of polarization states that, depending upon the type of personality, frustrations and misfortunes are reacted to and overcome, often by an increased creative effort (deafness of Beethoven, blindness of Milton, etc.) and by altruistic transformation (positive polarization); and often by suicide, mental disorder, brutalization, increase of selfishness, dumb submissiveness, and cynical sensualism (negative polarization). The same polarization occurs on a mass scale when catastrophes and frustrations fall upon a large collectivity. Some of its members become more aggressive, brutal, sensual (*carpe diem*), and otherwise mentally and morally disintegrated, while the other part of the collectivity becomes more religious, moral, altruistic, and saintly, as shown also by our "catastrophic altruists." This law explains why periods of catastrophe are marked by disintegration of the value-system of a given society, and by growth of demoralization, criminality, wars, and bloody revolts, on one hand; and on the other, by a creative reintegration of a new value-system, especially of religious and ethical values, and by spiritual and moral improvement of the positively polarized segment of the population. As a rule, all great religious and moral systems have emerged and then have been ennobled, mainly in catastrophic periods of a society, be it

Ancient Egypt, China, India, Israel, the Greco-Roman, or the Western nations.

The preceding chapter has shown that this polarization goes on also at the present time. The gigantic struggle between the forces of positive and negative polarization is the real struggle of our age. If in this fateful conflict the forces of positive polarization eventually prevail over those of negative polarization, all will be well with mankind. If the forces of demoralization and disintegration are victorious, then the future of humanity will become dark and uncertain. This tragic situation emphasizes once again the paramount importance of the task demanded from all of us by the present historical situation, of the altruistic transformation of mankind, and of the human universe.

E6